Bound 8/8/77

Equatorial Africa

JOSEPH C. MILLER

518 AHA PAMPHLETS
AMERICAN HISTORICAL ASSOCIATION
400 A Street, SE, Washington, D.C. 20003

JOSEPH C. MILLER is associate professor of history at the University of Virginia, where he has been since 1972. He has previously taught at the University of Wisconsin—Madison. He received his B.A. from Wesleyan University and his M.A. and Ph.D. from the University of Wisconsin. His research interests are Central African history, especially Portuguese Africa, and the history of slavery and the slave trade. He is the author of *Kings and Kinsmen: Early Mbundu States in Angola* (Clarendon Press, 1976), "Requiem for the 'Jaga' " (*Cahiers d'études africaines*, 1973), "The Imbangala and the Chronology of early Central African History" (*Journal of African History*, 1972), and numerous other articles which have appeared in major historical journals in the United States, Canada, and Europe. He received a Foreign Area Fellowship for research in Africa in 1968–71, and has been awarded postdoctoral fellowships from the American Council of Learned Societies and the National Endowment for the Humanities.

Standard Book Number: 0-87229-021-2
Library of Congress Catalog Card Number: 76-42066

Composed and printed at The William Byrd Press, Inc.
Richmond, Virginia 23228
Printed in the United States of America

Equatorial Africa

JOSEPH C. MILLER

The forests and savannas of Equatorial Africa stretching east of the Cameroons toward the great African lakes and south to the Zambezi River remain for most Europeans and Americans the quintessential African heart of darkness, vast and empty expanses isolated from the mainstream of world history. A few Equatorial Africans have in fact cherished their relative remoteness, and some have preserved small-scale autonomous societies down to nearly the present day, pioneering in the creation of original political and economic, artistic and social forms, almost entirely without the advantages associated with even restricted literacy. But for centuries before the earliest surviving evidence of their achievements, most people in Equatorial Africa maintained widespread and intimate contact with one another through extensive and complex political, economic, and social institutions. That Europeans have known little or nothing about Equatorial Africa does not mean that the area has been isolated from the rest of the world. The fact is, Equatorial Africans have been in touch with other parts of the world for nearly as long as their history records. The barriers that restricted Equatorial Africa's commerce with other parts of the world gave the region a history of its own, with distinctive themes and a periodization that only partly paralleled the major movements in African or global history. It is the intent of this pamphlet to outline the regionally coherent themes that link the separate histories of the hundreds of states and kingdoms, commercial networks, and village and lineage units that have appeared there in past centuries.

3

One of the important reasons why Equatorial African history has remained shrouded in obscurity among Europeans derives from the difficulty of developing a Euro-American style "history," which has traditionally depended on written documents, from the other kinds of evidence available for most of the Equatorial African past, at least before the present century. The absence of literacy in Equatorial Africa led Western historians to regard themselves as capable of reconstructing only the small part of Equatorial Africa's past illuminated by European records. Since these records covered mainly the activities of Europeans along parts of the Atlantic coast and in adjacent portions of the interior from the early sixteenth century until the latter nineteenth century and only spread to cover virtually the entire area by the second or third decade of the present century, historians studied little more than the history of Europeans in Africa. This truncated and restricted sort of history yielded during the past twenty years to a new generation of historians, of whom the most innovative and accomplished practitioner in Equatorial Africa has been Professor Jan Vansina. These historians are sensitive to the historical value of African verbal arts— oral traditions, proverbs, songs, and so on, and to the potential of linguistic data, ethnographic materials, and other less conventional forms of evidence from the past. With more sophisticated historical techniques, the topical focus of historical studies in Equatorial Africa swung decisively from colonial and imperial history to the history of African politicians, merchants, and warlords. Most recently, Equatorial African historiography has tended to abandon its former concentration on the activities of the wealthy and powerful few and to turn toward the vastly more numerous villagers, farmers, and artisans as subjects. This movement has flowed in large part from so-called resistance studies modeled on the seminal works of Professor Terence O. Ranger and has now matured into two distinct streams, one devoted to the social history of religion and the other to agricultural history. For the present, every sort of history in Equatorial Africa threatens constantly to topple from a firm basis in the available facts: the data are too few, the techniques for handling unconventional sources too new, the proportion of African societies yet studied too small, and the questions being posed too numerous and complex to allow more than provisional answers. The outline of themes and events that follows must be

4

understood in terms of this sweeping qualification, particularly for earlier periods, even though technical problems and the proper reservations have not been made explicit other than in these introductory remarks.

This essay brings internal dimensions of historical change in Equatorial Africa to the foreground and relegates themes deriving from European and Muslim contact to a secondary plane. The hope, in so doing, is to sketch out a predominately local perspective which approximates that of most Equatorial Africans at most times in the past. Such an approach is consistent with current interest in the "history of the many" and reflects the needs of Western readers who are familiar with European history and hardly require added stress on European events touching Africa but may find their perspectives broadened by an emphasis on continuities and tensions seen, as it were, from within Africa.

The major thematic emphasis falls on the emergence of variously specialized economies and stratified social groups from the relatively unspecialized and egalitarian bands of hunters and gatherers and the less differentiated communities of farmers who once lived in the central African savannas and forests. The history of kingdoms and nation-states centers on the conflicts that inevitably broke out among their constituent elements as some groups sought to establish their own hegemony over others or to defend their autonomy. New ideas and new technologies, taken in a broad sense to include administrative techniques as well as metallurgy and weaponry, defined the major periods of Equatorial African history as seen from this perspective: agriculture, metals, techniques of rule, literacy, and bureaucracy and modern weapons. The resulting periods, with approximate dates, are as follows:

The background of hunting and gathering	To beginning of the first millennium B.C.
Iron Age farming and fishing	Beginning of first millennium B.C. to 1200 A.D.
The time of kings	
1. States based on local resources	A.D. 1200 to 1500–1600 in some regions adjacent to the coast, lasting until 1800 in parts of the interior

2. Political structures heavily reliant on outside resources	1600–1800 to 1900–20, with a few surviving to the present
Commercial elites and warlords	
1. African, Muslim, and others	1800–80
2. European	1880–1920
Technocratic rule	
1. Colonial administrations	1920–59
2. Nationalist interlude	1960–65
3. Authoritarian	1965–present

The historical literature to date has covered primarily the second type of African state and the various literate elites here called "nationalists," but the approach taken up in this essay expands the historical horizon to include the vast majority of Equatorial Africans who have always been farmers, fishermen, and laborers, and it is intended to provide a framework for the integration of intellectual, religious, social, and economic history of all the people who have lived in Equatorial Africa.

The Background of Hunting and Gathering

History in Equatorial Africa took shape against a background of Stone Age hunters and gatherers engaged in the slow refinement of a relatively undifferentiated Paleolithic (or early Stone Age) technology toward more specialized Neolithic (or late Stone Age) industries that became carefully adapted to the natural resources of the regions where each band lived.[1] In general these bands adapted their tools to three basic Equatorial African environments—a riverain ecology found along major watercourses or around the shores of lakes and ponds, the moist tropical rain forest with its hardwoods and small fauna, and the more open savannas with their diversity of large game living in grasslands,

Many basic references, unpublished and in languages other than English, included in the original draft of this pamphlet have been eliminated from the published footnotes in the interest of reducing the overall dimensions of the essay. In general, works have been mentioned only once, where they first become relevant, and not in subsequent sections dealing with the same areas or topics. Readers interested in acquiring a more detailed bibliography will find most of the eliminated references cited in the works mentioned.

[1] For Equatorial Africa, as for the rest of the continent, the best introduction to the Stone Age is J. Desmond Clark, *The Prehistory of Africa* (New York, 1970). Roland Oliver and Brian M. Fagan, *Africa in the Iron Age* (Cambridge, 1975), 22–32, provide a judicious synthesis of more recent work.

woods, and gallery forests along the rivers. The great equatorial forest blanketed the land from the shores of the Atlantic eastward to the great African lakes within about five degrees on either side of the equator. To the north, a relatively narrow band of rolling forest-savanna mosaic with marked annual alternation of wet and dry seasons extended only to the watershed between the Ubangi River tributaries and those of the Logone and Shari to the west and the affluents of the Bahr-el-Ghazal in the east. Beyond stretched the drier Sudanic regions that later belonged more to western or Saharan Africa than to Equatorial Africa. South of the forest the savannas formed a broad east-west band drained by streams flowing to the Zaïre (formerly Congo) River system and by the Zambezi and its major northern tributaries, the Kafue and the Luangwa. Near the Atlantic the Ogowe drained the forested regions, and farther south the Kwanza, the Kunene, and other smaller rivers flowed down from the most mountainous highlands found in the predominantly rolling terrain of the region. Beyond the southern savannas stretched the drier steppes that eventually merged into the Kalahari Desert.

From available archaeological evidence and from comparison with surviving Stone Age peoples, specialists surmise that the forest dwellers tended to be relatively small and light skinned and lived in bands of thirty to fifty individuals. Their pursuit of game kept them on the move in a carefully calculated cycle of their hunting grounds, and so they constructed only temporary shelters of leaves and poles, quite adequate in a life in which more permanent structures would have been worse than useless. Their diet probably drew about equally on vegetable and animal sources of nourishment, with the men specialized in hunting game and the women occupied in foraging nearer their camps. They had little occasion for intensive contact with strangers or for exploration beyond the confines of their own territories, but in their isolation they developed delicately balanced social relationships allowing essential group decisions to be taken without the guidance of defined leaders and the refined moral, ethical, and artistic sensitivities of their modern descendants, the Pygmies.[2]

Savanna-dwelling hunters and gatherers led similarly mobile

[2] For the Bambuti Pygmies of the northeastern Belgian Congo in the 1950s, see the sympathetic and sensitive portrayal by Colin Turnbull, *The Forest People* (New York, 1961).

lives but specialized in the hunting of large ruminants—giraffe, many species of antelope, elephant, zebra, warthog, and buffalo—and in the collection of wild cereals that grew in their grassy plains. In particularly favorable circumstances, known from camps located on the banks of the Kafue affluent of the Zambezi since around 2500 B.C., savanna dwellers of this period might congregate in groups of up to three hundred or more during the rainy season when vegetation was lush and game plentiful. They dispersed in groups of thirty to one hundred during the dry months to hunt with bows and arrows, throwing-sticks, poison, and game pits. Their contacts with their neighbors had intensified to the point that a method of defining respective territories had emerged, and exotic shells, stones, and probably other less durable items were passed in sporadic trade over distances of hundreds of miles.[3] History, for all of these people, consisted not in the rise and fall of empires but in the gradual refinement of hunting techniques, a steady spread of superior inventions from one band to another, and probably in a corresponding slow growth in population, although always at levels much below the densities achieved later by farmers.

Iron Age Farming and Fishing

Fishermen like those known to have lived in the Kafue Valley at about the same time first developed the technology that permitted sedentary life, opened the door to the development of architecture and larger-scale social and political organization, intensified trade, and presumably ended the egalitarianism of the hunters and gatherers. Fish traps, nets, and spears allowed these people to support themselves from the rivers without constant movement in pursuit of game, while the higher nutritional yields available from fishing supported denser populations. The cooperative labor necessary for efficient fishing encouraged people to settle in larger and more compact villages composed of more substantial dwellings. The larger scale of social organization must have required some sort of centralized coordination, perhaps achieved through reliance on the good judgment of experienced elders, or

---

[3] Creighton Gabel, *Stone Age Hunters of the Kafue: The Gwisho A Site* (Boston, 1965), provides an introduction easily understood by the nonspecialist. Brian M. Fagan, in *A Short History of Zambia* (London, 1966), ch. 4, places Gwisho in the broader perspective of the later Stone Age in Zambia.

through the wisdom of a single arbitrator or judge. Ambitious and successful individuals could for the first time amass greater wealth in the form of nets, fish traps, canoes, and houses than their less fortunate kinsmen and neighbors. These fishermen probably dried fish to exchange for vegetable products and game available from their hunter-gatherer neighbors, giving rise to local commercial networks that in turn introduced isolated bands of foragers to pots made by the fishermen from river clays, brought new and exotic products to isolated bands, and contributed to the diffusion of technical innovations and of ideas throughout ever larger regions. The fishermen thus exercised a crucial influence on the critical transition from the slow development characteristic of hunting and gathering societies to the more rapid historical changes that followed.

The first specifically identifiable events of Equatorial African history involved the spread of a new fishing and planting culture from the northwest and its diffusion and differentiation throughout almost the entire region. Over the course of several hundred years these aboriginal fishermen, now called Bantu, brought the first cultigens to Equatorial African and introduced the fundamental ideological perspectives of its modern inhabitants. They spread languages ancestral to most of the African languages spoken there today and may have significantly altered the genetic character of the population toward the so-called Negro type prevalent there now. The most plausible—though still speculative—description of how the Bantu accomplished all this begins well before the opening of the first millennium B.C., near the Benue River in the West African savannas. People living there fished with dugout canoes, nets, fishhooks, and other equipment in standard use among Neolithic African fishermen. They lived in fairly large and compact settlements, accorded some authority to councils of lineage elders, traced descent through women (thus young people owed primary obedience to their uncles, or brothers of their mothers, rather than to their fathers). They cultivated some common early West African food crops (yams, oil palms), and raised goats. From their superior agricultural and stockkeeping technology these Bantu achieved greater population densities, lived in larger settlements, and had an ability to survive drought or misfortune that people in and south of the forest lacked. For reasons not known with certainty but usually

9

attributed to population pressures building along the Benue as Saharan farmers drifted south to escape increasing dryness during the second millennium B.C., some of the Bantu fishermen moved away from their overcrowded homelands, traversed the northern savanna, and after a long delay reached the Zaïre tributaries that opened an all-water route toward the Zambezi and beyond.

The ensuing spread of Bantu languages and culture throughout the forest and across the southern savanna probably required more than a thousand years to complete and can hardly be termed a "Bantu migration," as much of the secondary literature has described the process. Bantu technological superiority allowed small groups to overcome their relatively impoverished neighbors and to enter into periods of local population growth. As their fishing settlements grew beyond the size at which the inhabitants could efficiently and peacefully work together, dissidents emigrated toward the south and east, perhaps not more than a few miles away from the crowded rivers behind them. There they settled again and began anew the cycle of prosperity and growth leading to further segmentation and expansion in later generations.

The slowly advancing Bantu speakers undoubtedly dispersed some of the local fishermen and intermarried with others who learned the language and customs of the newcomers. Some of the Pygmy hunters of the densest forests retreated from the Bantu and preserved their ancient way of life into the present era, expecially in upper Gabon and in the Ituri forest of northeastern Zaïre; intermittent contact with Bantu settlements often led even the Pygmies eventually to adopt Bantu languages. Pockets of hunter-gatherers in the southern savannas preserved their own way of life until as recently as the last century. Elsewhere the double process of population growth among the newcomers and the assimilation of local inhabitants into Bantu society spread their languages and cultures slowly throughout Equatorial Africa except in the northern grasslands where, in still badly understood movements, former Saharan and Sudanic farmers moved south as they retreated from dessication in the desert.

The originally homogeneous Bantu mixed with indigenous populations and adapted Bantu language and culture to local environments to produce the diversity of material cultures, artistic traditions, ideologies, and the over four hundred distinct Bantu

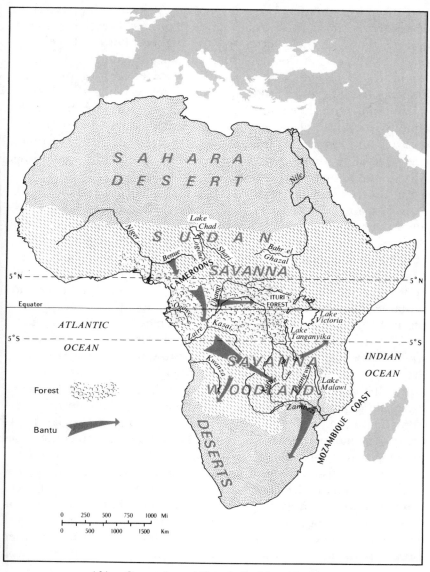

Africa: Geography and Hypothesized Spread of Bantu

languages known today. Some of the eastern groups acquired cattle and sheep from herders living in the East African highlands, while others in the southern savannas developed the cultivation of millet and sorghum as they populated the higher plains between the rivers. With agriculture and settlement came a tendency to organize in terms of comprehensive lineage systems, with marriage, descent, and inheritance rights predominately calculated according to affiliation with the relatives of one parent or the other but rarely equally with both; life generally concentrated on the local problems of crops and kinsmen.[4] This process, repeated thousands of times over several centuries, began the evolution toward the Equatorial African ethnolinguistic groups identifiable today.

But the trend toward differentiation of the aboriginal Bantu stock of words and ideas was countered by a simultaneous tendency toward homogenization. These new ideas and innovations kept Bantu settlements in contact with one another through the movements of fishermen and traders up and down the rivers; they carried novelties that hastened the replacement of stone, wood, and bone techniques with rudimentary iron knives, hoes, and axes and explained new notions of religion and politics. By the nineteenth century this process had resulted in a segmented commercial network of transcontinental proportions and reinforced the common stratum of culture underlying the entire Bantu-speaking region.

A variety of new techniques penetrated Equatorial Africa in the first millennium A.D. via maritime contacts linking eastern Africa to the Arabian peninsula, India, and southeastern Asia. Knowledge of iron smelting and of at least two important southeast Asian food crops—the banana and taro, a kind of starchy root crop equivalent to our potato—spread to Bantu advancing toward the Rift Valley and perhaps also among others who descended the Zambezi toward the Indian Ocean. Since these cultigens thrived in moist climates and increased the caloric yield of agriculture relative to Bantu practices of that time, the fishermen in the forested regions were able to move away from the rivers into the clearings in the forest. Sophistication in the working of iron spread in at least two

---

[4] A stimulating theoretical discussion of the relationships between environment, technology, and social organization applicable to the early history of Equatorial Africa appears in Robin Horton, "Stateless Societies in the History of West Africa," in J. F. A. Ajayi and Michael Crowder, eds., *History of West Africa* (New York, 1971), 1:78–119.

major waves—initially in an early first millennium diffusion of simple smelting techniques capable of producing small and brittle iron tools only marginally superior to implements already in use. The second wave, between 700 and 1200 A.D., introduced a shaft-type furnace able to maintain high smelting temperatures with a great degree of control and precision; this established Equatorial African Iron Age technologies much as they remained a millennium later. The forest Bantu seem to have developed this innovation on the basis of excellent charcoal produced from local hardwoods. For the first time the Equatorial African Bantu were able to manufacture heavy broad-bladed tools and weapons with which they created material cultures before about 1200 that became the antecedents of those that lasted into the present century. Since it may be presumed that the associated social structures and attitudes also stabilized in something like their modern form at about the same time, the end of the twelfth century roughly marks the crystallization of social and cultural groups that, however they might rise and fall or expand and contract, endured as the basic framework of Equatorial African history for the next seven hundred years.[5]

The Time of Kings

States based on local resources

The two or three centuries after 1200 A.D. saw the related but distinct development of kings and commerce in Equatorial Africa. During this period the ancient merchants of the lower Zaïre and the lower Ogowe developed a coast-hinterland trade while those along the upper Zambezi intensified their contacts with traders from the Indian Ocean. The complex commerce of the Sahara, which had touched the northern savannas lightly since classical antiquity, continued, and imperial developments around Lake Chad in this period probably resulted in the northward sale of a few undesired kinsmen from that area as slaves.

[5] The lengthy and technical debate on the evidence for the spread of Bantu languages and their possible association with the movements of people, the distribution of artifacts and ideas has been succinctly summarized in Philip D. Curtin, *Precolonial African History,* AHA Pamphlets 501 (Washington, 1974), 31–35. The best historical reconstruction is Jan Vansina, "Inner Africa," in *The Horizon History of Africa* (New York, 1971), 2:261–66. Christopher Ehret, David Dalby, and D. W. Phillipson carry on the debate in the *Journal of African History, Transafrican Journal of History,* and *Ufahamu* volumes for 1974, 1975, and 1976.

Within and just south of the forest, Zaïre River traders helped to distribute imports from all three sources to every corner of the region and undoubtedly sold their own excellent iron, steel, and other forest products to the inhabitants of the savannas.

The origins of political centralization in Equatorial Africa lay in aggregations of strangers who crowded together at centers of rare natural resources—salt pans, copper outcrops, or exposed deposits of iron ores—vital to the economies of the villagers of the forests and grasslands. Most Iron Age settlements tended toward economic self-sufficiency, as their women grew cereals in fields located on lineage lands and their men hunted for meat primarily in the surrounding woods and meadows. Few, however, possessed sources of iron ore on their own lands, although everyone depended on iron hoes to work the root-bound soil and iron axes to fell the trees covering it. Most could procure a salty ash by burning saline grasses but preferred the purer salt obtained from infrequent saline marshes or coastal salt pans. Copper, desired for ornaments and invested with supernatural properties, was still more rare. Networks of kinship and affinity linked most villagers to their immediate neighbors and were adequate to regulate ordinary local commerce, as well as dry season communal hunts and the exchange of women as wives, but were of little avail to individuals who ventured to mines or trade centers located outside the neighborhood in which they lived.

Since the institutions of kinship could not maintain order among the unrelated strangers who congregated around the salt pans and copper and iron mines, it is not unlikely that independent market place officials assumed the authority to police the conduct of trade in these unregulated, disorderly, and dangerous centers. Some Equatorial African salt pans and mines presumably became neutral territory in terms of local lineage politics, but in others individuals or groups managed to control the resource in their own interests. A wide variety of circumstances—a fortuitous superiority in manpower, the energy of a skilled and ambitious individual, or the artful handling of effective charms or new weapon technology—could have allowed one group or another to restrict access to its copper, iron or salt. The twelfth-century spread of more effective iron-smelting techniques and intensification of trade with the outside world must have created multiple opportunities for the emer-

14

gence of powerful and wealthy individuals who, for the first time, asserted political—that is, nonkinship—authority over previously autonomous lineages.

The idea of a nonlineage form of authority must have existed in many parts of Equatorial Africa since remote periods, and one may assume that many symbols and ideologies of such authority circulated in the second half of the first millennium. Occasionally some new symbol or idea in the hands of a creative person grew from a village emblem to stand for a small kingdom; some of these proto-states survived for many years, but many others grew only to decline at once, leaving no more trace than a distorted rumor picked up by sixteenth-century European mariners or an amorphous recollection in modern oral traditions. The earliest archaeological evidence of the presence of states comes from eighth- or ninth-century fishing towns on the shores of the northern Shaba lakes.[6] Political symbols and ideologies spread in all directions, with inspiration sometimes coming along the trade routes from other parts of Africa, as in the case of a certain type of clapperless bell originally from the vicinity of modern Nigeria or in the instance of influences north of the Zambezi from early Shona kingdoms on the Rhodesian plateau.[7] There is too little evidence to speculate on the history of kings who failed, but the most enduring successes seem to have occurred in three, or perhaps four, areas—the Shaba lake region, the central Zaïre lakes, the north side of the lower Zaïre River, and perhaps the central Angolan high plateau. All four centers may date from the thirteenth century or earlier.

The northern Shaba complex, which probably descended from eighth- and ninth-century lake fishermen, may be taken as the oldest of the four. In Shaba peoples ancestral to a widespread group later known as Luba elaborated a political ideology based on the notion of *bulopwe*—in political terms a hereditary right to interfere in the affairs of persons unrelated to the *bulopwe*-holder. Although this notion spread widely through the southern savannas, in part, perhaps, through *bulopwe*-holders' manipulation of marriage alliances and in part by resettlement of *bulopwe*-holders and their

[6] Jean Hiernaux, Emma Maquet, and Josse de Buyst, "Excavations at Sanga, 1958: A First Millennium Civilization on the Upper Lualaba," *South African Journal of Science*, 64 (1968):113–17.

[7] Jan Vansina, "The Bells of Kings," *Journal of African History*, 10, 2 (1969):187–98; Harry W. Langworthy, *Zambia before 1890: Aspects of Pre-Colonial History* (London, 1972), 11–12.

15

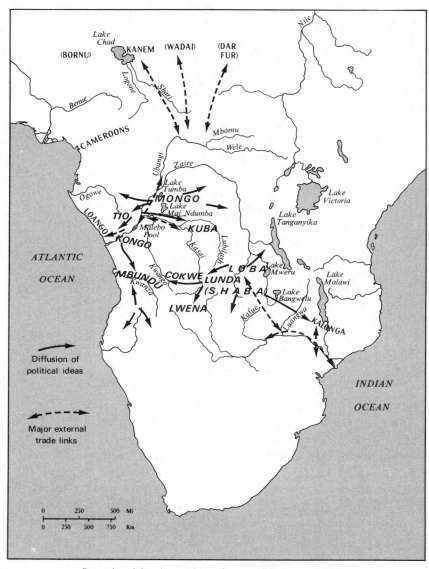

Central and Southern Africa: Centers of Equatorial African
Political Innovation, before 1500

entourages. Few early *bulopwe* heirs enjoyed extensive power, and their ideology and symbols proved useful primarily as means of formalizing existing relationships not comprehended by the prevailing kinship calculus. In the nontechnological society of the time, where rudimentary weapons and administrative technology conferred little power, only superiority in manpower could provide one person or descent group with the means to dominate another. The institution of slavery made wealth convertible into retainers, but limitations on accumulating substantial riches in the absence of salt pans or regular contacts with Indian Ocean merchants kept all but a few from building retinues large enough to impose their wills consistently on their neighbors. This decentralized and gradual political development, perhaps related to large-scale population movements in regions where ecological conditions or raiding produced demographic change, modified lineage politics southeast beyond the Luangwa and northeast toward the Lubilash perhaps as early as the thirteenth century, and left a widespread heritage of common Luba political culture throughout the southern savannas.[8]

The next stage in Luba political history began when a few *bulopwe*-holders raised themselves to the status of kings in the sense that they could demand respect, tribute, and obedience on a continuing basis from the less prestigious or wealthy *bulopwe*-holders around them. Oral traditions pick up the development of such hierarchically organized networks of titles at an unknown date[9] just northwest of the northern Shaba lakes with the metaphorical story of Kalala Ilunga, a noble *bulopwe*-holder remembered as the founder of the "first Luba empire."[10] Meanwhile, a shadowy kingdom known as Kalonga developed at the southern end of Lake Malawi; it was ideologically related to the Luba of Katanga and probably grew as one result of augmented trade flowing north from

[8] This interpretation of early Luba political history is consistent with later and presumably analogous historical processes documented elsewhere (chapters by Alagoa and Smith in Ajayi and Smith, *History of West Africa,* 1) but challenges the established historiography on the early Katanga kingdoms, which has probably tended to overuse the mechanism of "migration" to explain these events.

[9] This date has traditionally been taken as around the sixteenth century, but it was probably much earlier. For a summary of the debate and for the argument in favor of substantially earlier dating, see Joseph C. Miller, "The Imbangala and the Chronology of Early Central African History," *Journal of African History,* 13, 4 (1972):549-74.

[10] Jan Vansina, *Kingdoms of the Savanna* (Madison, 1966), 71-78, summarizes the Luba traditions and mentions published sources.

17

the lower Zambezi valley where as many as ten thousand coastal Muslim traders may have established themselves before the end of the fifteenth century.[11] Although other kingdoms must have existed as well, too little evidence survives to identify them. None could have approached the size or degree of centralization achieved in later Equatorial African states.

A parallel evolution of decentralized political authority occurred just south of the forests of the central Zaïre basin in about the twelfth century. Riverain traders, related to the ancestors of people now known as Mongo, kept the people inhabiting the central Zaïre tributaries in regular contact with one another. One effect of this commerce was that the Mongo retained a greater degree of cultural homogeneity than their neighbors to the north and south. Another was that some of them began to recognize a special type of commercial arbiter called an *nkumu*. Neighboring Mongo lineages, like those of the Luba, maintained ties of kinship and affinity, but the wide-ranging river traders often dealt with strangers and must have needed some sort of local authority that could settle commercial disputes and judge the offenses against persons and property of which rivermen everywhere are occasionally guilty. In the commercialized and capitalistic atmosphere along these rivers this role fell to the wealthiest and most successful traders, thus creating a decentralized plutocracy of *nkumu* chiefs that spread throughout the region. *Nkumu* increased their power and created permanent courts and dynasties only at the southwestern fringe of the Mongo area near Lake Mai-Ndumba (formerly Lac Léopold II). The symbols and ideology of this form of the *nkumu* diffused among the central Mongo and later moved west across the Zaïre River as far as the headwaters of the Ogowe.[12]

In the third center of political innovation, two kingdoms appeared before 1500 among Kongo and Tio on the north side of the lower Zaïre River. Tio living northwest of Malebo Pool (formerly Stanley Pool) gradually conceded allegiance to a single line of lord-kings, probably the heirs of predecessors who earlier had introduced improved iron-smelting techniques along with fragments of Mongo

[11] For Kalonga, see Langworthy, *Zambia before 1890*, 29–30.
[12] Readers of English may consult Vansina, *Kingdoms of the Savanna*, 99–102, but a revised short summary appears in Jan Vansina, *Introduction à l'Ethnographie du Congo* (Brussels, n.d.), 79–92.

political terminology and ideology to the western savannas.[13] Related notions of political authority diffused from the Tio to Kongo-speaking lineages on the north bank of the Zaïre and from there to the southern Kongo living between the lower Kwango and the ocean. Centralization became more pronounced south of the river where a line of fourteenth- and fifteenth-century titleholders known as *mani kongo* incorporated other noble titleholders in a small kingdom.[14] The relatively uncentralized forms of Kongo and Tio political organization succumbed to powerful lords who controlled an exchange of forest products for sea salt and shells that passed through market places located near Malebo Pool. Other Mongo-derived Tio political influences traveled up the Kasai, touching off incipient political organization among the river people up to the area beyond the confluence of the Sankuru. There a local clan, the Bushoong, began to create the central institutions of what later became the Kuba kingdom.

Although little is yet known in detail of pre-1500 Equatorial African political development outside these three centers, events seem generally to have followed the flow of trade and the diffusion of political institutions. Small trading and fishing communities located on the bays of the coast north of the Zaïre may have brokered a limited commerce in copper and other produce of the interior obtained from Tio, Kongo, and Mongo on the one hand and sold to peoples from the Cameroons and eastern Nigeria; in return, they added their own salt and dried fish to sales of imports from the north.[15] The peoples of the northern savanna presumably traded with their Sudanic neighbors to the north and west. They may have become victims of slave raiding emanating from the states of the central and eastern Sudan—Wadai, Kanem, Bornu, and Dar Fur—but no political developments are discernible. To the southwest of the Luba as far as the Kwanza River lived a broad band of

[13] For this and following discussions of the Tio, see Jan Vansina, *The Tio Kingdom of the Middle Congo, 1880–1892* (London, 1973), 439–43. See also Vansina, "Probing the Past of the Lower Kwilu Peoples (Zaïre)," *Paideuma,* 19/20 (1973–74):332–64.

[14] Accounts in English include Vansina, *Kingdoms of the Savanna,* 36–40; Georges Balandier, *Daily Life in the Kingdom of the Kongo* (New York, 1968), 27–41; and David B. Birmingham, *Trade and Conflict in Angola* (Oxford, 1966), 1–9.

[15] Historians writing on this part of the coast have tended, though with little basis in evidence, to project the large kingdoms of the seventeenth century back to earlier periods. The standard account is Phyllis Martin, *The External Trade of the Loango Coast, 1576–1870* (Oxford, 1972), 1–32. K. David Patterson, *The Northern Gabon Coast to 1875* (Oxford, 1975) indicates directions in which future research is likely to move.

19

people organized in matrilineages who may have received very early but attenuated Luba influences. These in any case produced little centralization except among the Lunda nearest to the emerging Luba kingdoms. There an unstratified federation of Lunda titleholders moved toward increasingly centralized and hierarchical political institutions and simultaneously exported Lunda political ideology to the south and west. The spread of Lunda political institutions, perhaps in part through movements of Lunda emigrants but certainly also through the borrowing of their ideas by local populations, left the Lwena of the upper Zambezi and Cokwe within the bend of the Kasai with uncentralized networks of Lunda titleholders. Echoes of the Kongo smith-king complex reverberated in less centralized form among the Mbundu of the lower Kwanza. On the high plateau southwest of them a fourth center of political innovation may have materialized among highland farmers and herders who linked their kings with cattle, but the evidence on this point is too problematic to merit more than passing reference at present.[16]

The primary theme of Equatorial African history during the three centuries after 1200 A.D. was the halting development of political institutions capable of settling disputes and coordinating the efforts of individuals and groups not related under the prevailing systems of kinship. The three, and perhaps four, centers of innovation witnessed the formulation of new ideas and symbols of kingship that spread as parochial-minded people adopted and modified them to regulate the disorder attending the breakdown of the historic isolation of their lineages. In most cases, certainly among the Mongo and probably among the Luba and the Tio/Kongo, the forces drawing lineages into ever-widening contacts hinged on commerce—the exchange of local products among the forests, savannas, lakes, and seacoasts of Equatorial Africa as well as increasingly between Equatorial Africans and Muslims from the Indian Ocean, western and northern Africans in the

[16] On the Lunda and other southwestern matrilineal groups, see Vansina, *Kingdoms of the Savanna*, 78–83, and Birmingham, *Trade and Conflict in Angola*, 10–17. A revisionist account is Joseph C. Miller, *Kings and Kinsmen: Early States among the Mbundu of Angola* (Oxford, 1976), ch. 5. A new synthesis for this and the following period is David Birmingham, "Central Africa from Cameroun to the Zambezi," in Richard Gray, ed., *The Cambridge History of Africa* (Cambridge, 1975), 4:325–83. These authorities underlie all following discussions of these regions.

northern savannas, and perhaps west Africans near the Atlantic coast. With our fragmentary knowledge of the centuries between 1200 and 1500, only vague remnants and tantalizingly unexpected ethnographic distributions hint at other proto-kingdoms that may have crumbled before they reached maturity and at areas of intellectual and social history that remain to be reconstructed.

Political structures heavily reliant on outside resources

The sixteenth century initiated a new era in Equatorial African history in three interrelated senses. First, its western and far southeastern regions experienced intensified commercial activity along the existing routes down the Zambezi and along the lower Zaïre, with secondary effects that reached far inland. With the new economic currents, new groups rose within the established ethno-linguistic configurations. Some localities gained advantages relative to others, and in some cases kings benefited from the changes to bring their states to new levels of centralization and penetration into the underlying lineage structure. A secondary change distinguishing the centuries after 1500 from those before was the presence of small groups of migrant Europeans, mainly Portuguese, at a few points along the Atlantic coast and their infiltration of the Arab trading system along the lower Zambezi. At the beginning, the Europeans had no technological advantages and too few men to rout the kings of Equatorial Africa on the field of battle, but their command of the seas, their ability to coordinate far-flung activities and resources through their use of writing, and a material culture based on firearms and rapidly growing more sophisticated gradually overcame their tendency to succumb to tropical diseases. They managed to establish one small state, Angola, that maintained stable commercial and diplomatic relations with surrounding African kingdoms. More significant than their limited political and military accomplishments was their role as transporters within Africa and between Equatorial Africa and the labor- and raw material-hungry economies of Europe and the Americas. Overseas demand for African manpower and for such commodities as ivory, gums, dyewoods, and gold, as well as intra-African trade, significantly influenced most of the social and political changes of this period. The third but minor sense in which 1500 marked a change in Equatorial African history was that Europeans left the first written record of events on its fringes—Kongo, Angola, and the regions southeast of the Luangwa. Written records obviously did not alter the course of history but did create a record of certain aspects of it for the first time.

Three Portuguese caravels inaugurated the new era when they dropped anchor off the Kongo kingdom in 1483. The *mani kongo* Nzinga Nkuwu welcomed them and converted to Christianity a few years later. He renamed his capital São Salvador and accepted Portuguese artisans, teachers, missionaries, and advisers at his court. Most Portuguese who went to Kongo subverted the professedly altruistic desires of their monarchs in Lisbon by initiating a trade in slaves and by meddling in Kongo politics against the interests of the kings. In Equatorial Africa, slavery and slave trading—hardly more than techniques of labor recruitment in an unmonetized economy—were politically sensitive institutions, for they were the critical means by which kings achieved their margin of superior manpower in societies without complex arms or extremes of material wealth. The entry of European slave-traders into Kongo labor markets at first reinforced royal authority, since they drew on the pool of slaves available through the Kongo kings. But European demands for slaves quickly exhausted limited royal reserves of dependents, and Portuguese merchants began to favor provincial nobles as they spread into every corner of the kingdom in search of more captives. By the middle of the sixteenth century, newly wealthy provincial lords were in rebellion against the *mani kongo*, and a populace unwilling to endure continued kidnapping and disorder was on the verge of revolt. Later *mani kongo* managed to reunite the provinces of the old kingdom only temporarily as the Kongo returned to a smaller scale of political organization based no longer on lineages but on entourages of unrelated dependents clustered around members of a new class of traders grown wealthy on the trade in slaves.[17]

Elsewhere the first century of intensified commerce produced few effects as far-reaching as those that shook the Kongo, since no other African king incorporated Europeans at the center of a state and

---

[17] Vansina, *Kingdoms of the Savanna*, 41–69, 130–34, 138–42, 147–54. Also W. G. L. Randles, *L'Ancien royaume du Congo* (Paris, 1968), and Joseph C. Miller, "Requiem for the 'Jaga'," *Cahiers d'études africaines*, 13 (no. 49) (1973):121–49.

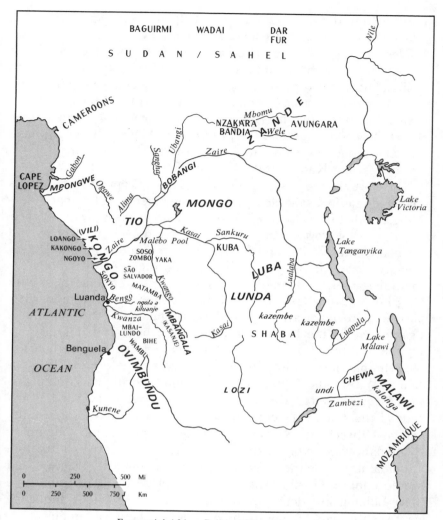

Equatorial Africa: Political History, 1500–1800

the Portuguese elsewhere tended to insinuate themselves into established patterns of intra-African trade.[18] Portuguese ships calling along the Loango coast contributed to the growth of a few prosperous villages at Kakongo, Ngoyo, and Loango into small trading states based on Kongo political models. The gradual intensification

[18] David Birmingham, "Early African Trade in Angola and Its Hinterland," in Richard Gray and David Birmingham, eds., *Pre-Colonial African Trade* (London, 1970), 163–73.

23

of trade from the Zambezi may have helped a brief expansion of the Malawi kingdom and it converted the *undi*, a line of related title-holders among the Chewa to the west, from minor chieftains to increasingly powerful kings in their own right.[19] Although the political balance north of Malebo Pool did not change significantly, New World food crops—maize, peanuts, manioc, beans, and others—had spread up the Kasai as far as the Kuba by the 1620s, where they contributed to the production of agricultural surpluses that permitted the elaboration of Bushoong political institutions into a growing Kuba state.

The slave trade spread into new areas as European slave traders depleted readily available reserves of dependents in developed slaving grounds and as political instability grew in the wake of their raids. Private Portuguese merchants abandoned the Kongo and opened commercial relations with an emerging Mbundu king near the Kwanza, the *ngola a kiluanje*. A Portuguese royal donatory mounted a series of small-scale military interventions there after 1575 but had few victories until his successors joined forces after 1610 with roving warriors called Imbangala. The large numbers aggregated by the Imbangala bands and their tight military discipline, combined with the psychological effects of their claims to superhuman invincibility, made them extremely formidable opponents. Within the following decade, joint Portuguese-Imbangala armies overpowered the kingdom of the *ngola a kiluanje* and extended the sphere of Portuguese control some two hundred miles inland between the Kwanza and Bengo rivers. These sanguinary "Angolan wars" more than doubled the rate of slave exports from Luanda, and gave the Angolan slave trade its basic structure that would endure for more than two centuries—a ring of Imbangala slave-bulking kingdoms around the Portuguese colony funneling captives through Angola to the Americas. The most famous of the Imbangala states, Kasanje, located in the valley of the middle Kwango, became the largest single supplier of slaves in Equatorial Africa after 1650 when its kings agreed in principle to a commercial monopoly linking them to Portuguese governors and royally appointed slave contractors in Luanda. The old *ngola a kiluanje* kingdom disappeared but a remarkable woman ruler, the famous queen Nzinga, claimed the royal Mbundu title, adopted Imbangala tac-

[19] For this and subsequent references to the *undi*, Langworthy, *Zambia Before 1890*, ch. 5.

tics, and forged a new and powerful successor state in Matamba during the 1630s.[20]

The political geography of the highlands south of the Kwanza assumed its modern form in the sixteenth century as Imbangala lords in the region gradually established a set of kingdoms known as the Ovimbundu states. The largest of these—Mbailundo, Bihe, and Wambu—at first exported slaves to the Portuguese at Luanda but in the eighteenth century shifted to a secondary trading port some three hundred miles to the south at Benguela.[21]

The Equatorial African slave trade expanded to the Loango and Gabon coasts in the seventeenth century where it transformed the small coastal politics into kingdoms dominated by merchant princes. Loango, Kakongo, and Ngoyo thrived as powerful commercial organizations, small in geographical extent but extensive in terms of their traders' economic contacts; Vili or *mubire* from Loango fetched slaves all the way from the Tio south to the Mbundu. North of Cape Lopez, the Mpongwe near the Gabon River provisioned European shipping from western Africa and sold copper and iron, rafia cloths, red dyewoods, and miscellaneous charms and luxuries. The slave trade spread north of the Zaïre only after about 1660 and reached the Mpongwe around the middle of the eighteenth century. Trading groups similar to these formed among the western Kongo, or Sonyo, just south of the Zaïre and among the eastern Kongo, the Zombo or Soso, near the Kwango.

A brief outline of the structure of European slaving adds a more familiar dimension to the events just described in local terms. The sixteenth-century slave trade from this part of Africa was primarily in the hands of three competing groups of Portuguese: tax farmers and other appointees of Portuguese kings, a community of independent traders active in Kongo, and sugar planters and slave traders from the island of São Tomé just off Cape Lopez. Competition among them contributed to the disorders in Kongo and drove the losing São Tomé faction toward Luanda, where they

---

[20] I have summarized here my own interpretation of this period in Mbundu history as developed in *Kings and Kinsmen* and in "Nzinga of Matamba in a New Perspective," *Journal of African History*, 16, 2 (1975):201–16. Readers should also consult Vansina, *Kingdoms of the Savanna*, ch. 5, and Birmingham, *Trade and Conflict in Angola*.

[21] The early history of the Ovimbundu remains virtually unknown, despite the pioneering work of Gladwyn Childs, *Umbundu Kinship and Character* (London, 1949), for the eighteenth and nineteenth centuries.

began to buy slaves from the *ngola a kiluanje*. One reason for the establishment of a royal donatory at Luanda was the Portuguese monarchy's need to tax the trade pioneered by these renegades. Hostilities between officially sanctioned merchants and private traders, including Dutch as well as Portuguese, punctuated the Angolan wars of the seventeenth century. Losing factions repeatedly forsook established slaving areas to open the slave trade elsewhere, leading to the founding of Benguela and to Dutch development of the Loango slave trade after the Portuguese ended a brief Dutch occupation of Luanda from 1641 to 1648. French and English entered the trade at the end of the seventeenth century and helped to establish a rough competitive equilibrium that prevented any single European authority securing a monopoly that could contain the trade, thus contributing to its gradual but seemingly irresistible spread until by 1800 it had affected the entire coast from the Cameroons to the southern Angolan deserts.[22]

The Lunda political system expanded and parts of it became centralized during the seventeenth and eighteenth centuries as its kings, the *mwaant yaav*, grew powerful on their monopoly of initial Lunda contacts with European-oriented trade. Lineages as far west as the eastern banks of the Kwango came under the sway of nobles bearing Lunda titles during the seventeenth century, but few of these titleholders ever achieved significant political centralization, and many of them retained no more than formal ties to the central Lunda kingdom in western Shaba. During the 1740s secondary centers of Lunda political power formed in the east under nobles holding Lunda *kazembe* titles on the Lualaba salt pans and along the lower Luapula. The two *kazembe* enjoyed independent access to merchants from the lower Zambezi and in the later eighteenth century gained considerable autonomy and power by trading copper and other products with them. The *kiamfu* of the Yaka, the northernmost of the Lunda titles lining the Kwango, followed a parallel course toward centralization and autonomy through their access to Zombo merchants from Kongo. The *mwaant yaav* seem to have monopolized the crucial slave trade between Katanga and the

[22] Joseph C. Miller, "The Congo-Angola Slave Trade," in Martin L. Kilson and Robert I. Rotberg, eds., *The African Diaspora: Interpretive Essays* (Cambridge, Mass., 1976), 75–113.

middle Kwango kingdoms—Kasanje and others—from perhaps 1650 to 1800.[23]

The middle Zaïre fishermen and traders thrived on the intensified trade of this period but never supplemented their complex commercial networks with hierarchically ordered sets of political titles. Tio traders from Malebo Pool and along the lower Kasai spread up the Zaïre toward the Alima where they encountered a lower Ubangi community of traders known as Bobangi. Bobangi extended their commerce far into the forest and perhaps even up the Sangha toward the northern savannas, where they developed these contacts to become the most important traders of the middle river during the eighteenth century.

Intensified slave raiding also characterized the northern savannas in the eighteenth century. The sahel Muslim sultanates of Wadai, Dar Fur, Baguirmi, and Kanem-Bornu dispatched armed expeditions south to capture slaves among the small-scale societies of the savannas. People fleeing south, away from the raiders, contributed to population pressures in the northern forest and their effects, magnified in the limited cultivable spaces in the forest, forced some of the western Mongo to cross the middle Zaïre and ascend the Alima valley. In the east a military aristocracy arose to drive Muslim predators from the north away from Nzakara lineages living at the confluence of the Wele and Mbomu rivers. These warlords, called Bandia, also used their military skills to capture women from surrounding areas whom they awarded as wives to loyal followers, thus wresting control of the circulation of women from the lineages of their domains and encouraging local men to join the warlord's retinue. Their strategy fostered extreme centralization through the creation of colonies of loyal clients and dependents at their courts, by suppressing the significance of lineages, and by tying nearly every individual in their states personally to the kings. To the east an apparently local class of warlords called Vungara arose in imitation of the Bandia. The enforced movement of individuals through the Bandia and Vungara courts as retainers and wives homogenized the diverse languages and material cultures of the local peoples and began the formation of the extremely rich

[23] For the Lunda, see Vansina, *Kingdoms of the Savanna*, 160–74; Birmingham, *Trade and Conflict in Angola*, ch. 7; and Langworthy, *Zambia Before 1890*, chs. 3, 6. For the *kazembe*, see the work of Ian Cunnison, especially *History on the Luapula* (London, 1951).

27

and complex composite cultures of the peoples now known collectively as Zande.[24]

In the far southeast, the Chewa state of the *undi* drew strength from a seventeenth-century ivory trade with Portuguese settlements on the lower Zambezi. Its kings abandoned their formal subordination to the defunct Kalonga of the Malawi during the eighteenth century and spread subordinate titles among lineages from the Luangwa well southeast into the area of modern Mozambique.

In the upper Zambezi floodplain, an intricate economic network that included a great deal of population movement into and out of the river valley and complex interactions of farmers, fishermen, and cattle-herders as the floodwaters annually rose and receded, fostered the emergence of a single central authority to regulate relations between the strangers brought into frequent close contact. Local Lozi lineages combined Lunda-type political titles with a system of labor corvée based on regiments called *makolo* to form a number of small seventeenth-century chiefdoms with little overall centralization. One, or perhaps two, eighteenth-century titleholders gained control of *makolo* belonging to other chiefs. They expanded the ranks of the regimental commanders (known later as *induna*) and elevated them to the status of royal councillor and brought the entire valley and some of the surrounding highlands under unified rule.

The mature Lozi kingdom of the late eighteenth century had two capitals, one in the north and one in the south. It featured an elaborate balance of councils representing holders of the old Lunda political titles, several classes of councillors, and the central Lozi lineages. Merchants from southern Africa and Lwena slave raiders from the northwest both arrived at the end of the century; their trade with outlying councillors introduced divisive strains that weakened the dominant Lozi kings. The divergent pulls of commerce from the south and from the west exacerbated tensions

[24] The extensive publications of E. E. Evans-Pritchard on the "Zande" are not helpful for earlier historical periods; but see the studies collected in *The Azande: History and Political Institutions* (Oxford, 1971) on the Avungara regions. On the Bandia, the study of Eric de Dampierre, *Un ancien royaume Bandia du Haut-Oubangui* (Paris, 1967), has better historical sections. Northern savanna history is as yet little developed; for what is available, see Pierre Kalck, *Central African Republic* (New York, 1971), chs. 1, 2; and Pierre Alexandre, "Afrique centre-équatoriale et centre-occidentale," in Hubert Deschamps, ed., *Histoire Générale de l'Afrique Noire* (Paris, 1970), 1:353–67. These references serve for all following discussions of the northern savanna.

between the rival northern and southern capitals, further straining the kingdom's fragile unity.[25] The quality of life and the political and social institutions of many parts of Equatorial Africa in 1800 bore little resemblance to their predecessors of 1500 or so. The basic isolation of many lineages had opened to include intensified commerce and closer rule by distant kings. The relative demographic stability of earlier eras had disappeared in a shifting sea of populations in flight from the expanding slave trade; concomittantly, the multitude of small exchange economies continued to blend into four large commercialized systems, one facing down the Zambezi in the southeast, and others in the southwestern savannas, in the forest, and in the northern grasslands. Political ideologies based on notions originated before 1500 had diffused in all directions. But in some of the areas most affected by the slave trade the older kingdoms had already begun to undergo changes that foretold the shape of events to follow, as central kings, like those in Kongo, lost influence to wealthy new classes of traders grown rich on expanding commercial opportunities. Such kingdoms as the Lunda located far from the coastal sources of new wealth had not begun to reap the consequences of involvement in the slave trade by 1800 and were still consolidating on the strength of their kings' precarious commercial monopolies. Uncentralized populations in the northern savannas and in some Mongo areas dispersed before raiders emanating from the Sudan. Only a few parts of the region remained relatively untouched, mostly those in the economic shadows behind the large states, as in regions northwest of the *undi* kingdom or through most of the Luba domains where the *mwaant yaav*'s commercial monopolies and their own remoteness largely spared them the effects of direct involvement.

Commercial Elites and Warlords

African, Muslim, and others

Equatorial Africa eased unevenly from the era of trading kingdoms into an age dominated by foreign warlords commanding large armies of slave retainers, often employing military technology—weapons, tactics, and logistics—superior to that

[25] Mainga Mutumba, *Bulozi under the Luyana Kings* (London, 1973), chs. 1–4.

available to the established monarchs. Although the new lords followed the style of the Bandia warlords more than the subtle blend of lineage politics, magic, and coercion employed by the older lines of kings, ancient ideologies retained their strength and some states survived through the period, while in a few cases new classes seized power under the cover of the ancient titles. A pervasive phenomenon was intensified slaving flowing in part from British efforts after 1808 to end the Atlantic slave trade and the consequent deflection of most European slaving to Equatorial African coasts along the south Atlantic or into the Indian Ocean. At the same time, the need for agricultural labor by clove plantations on the East African islands of Pemba and Zanzibar propelled Muslim slavers beyond the great African lakes and into the eastern portions of Equatorial Africa. Developments in military technology and organization among minor Nguni chiefdoms in Natal eventually affected the northern side of the Zambezi with the penetration and settlement of hordes of migrating herdsmen and warriors. The resulting nineteenth-century warlord elites made Equatorial Africa more than ever an extension of the emerging worldwide economy, a supplier of labor to distant plantations and of raw materials to the industrializing nations of northwestern Europe and North America.

The ending of the Atlantic slave trade north of the equator increased slaving along the three existing commercial networks in the southern savannas and pushed them farther inland owing to the depletion of population strata available for sale near the coast. In general, the interior kingdoms recapitulated the sequence of initial centralization followed by dissolution that had first appeared in such coastal monarchies as the Kongo. Ivory, beeswax, palm products, rubber, and other exports replaced slaves on the trade routes to the coast after 1850, allowing independent nonaristocratic merchants to rise on the so-called legitimate trade but also giving a final impetus to the internal slave trade that supplied labor for the production and transportation of the new exports. By 1880, only a few of the older monarchies had preserved more than remnants of their former strength, while immigrant elites thrived in every quarter.

Along the trading system terminating at Kongo and Loango, the eighteenth-century Loango kingdoms first changed from centralized monarchies to oligarchies run by wealthy commercial brokers, then declined after 1860 as local producers of rubber and palm oil opened a host of new small ports along the coast. South of the Zaïre a similar profusion of small ports shipped beeswax, gum, and other products supplied by Sonyo and Zombo traders. Kongo politics remained decentralized, although remnants of the old Christian Kongo aristocracy still retained a certain prestige and occasionally made diplomatic contact with political or ecclesiastical authorities at Luanda.[26] Much of the produce exported along the Kongo and Loango coasts came from Bobangi and Tio trading settlements on the banks of Malebo Pool, the transshipment point linking the navigable interior basin of the Zaïre to the overland routes running down to the coast. The ancient Tio kings survived on the Tio plateau but shared their power with two new classes of lords—one composed of men claiming titles of nobility, the other of newly-rich but untitled merchants. Bustling trading villages along the river swelled with immigrants, who lived in commercial corporations led by wealthy traders rather than in lineages; one of the Bobangi dialects, Lingala, developed into a trade language reaching down to Malebo Pool by the 1880s.

To the south, Luanda's slave-producing hinterland retreated steadily away from the coast, enabling traders from Benguela, Loango, and Kongo to infiltrate regions that the main Portuguese merchant community had once regarded as its own. Luanda's share of the trade thus declined in a period of thriving commerce elsewhere on the coast, but the merchants there misdirected their efforts to recover prosperity into petitions for tax reform from Lisbon and into campaigns to drive French and British merchants off the coast. Vili and Kongo traders entered Kasanje in the early nineteenth century, broke the Kasanje kings' slaving monopoly and thereby contributed to a political fragmentation that culminated in civil wars during the 1850s. After 1850 wax and ivory replaced slaves as the bases of the Kasanje economy and enriched smaller-scale political authorities who built up slave retinues from the flow of captives formerly exported. Social institutions there followed the familiar shift from lineage-centered relationships to client commu-

[26] The most intensive work on this period of Kongo history, Susan Herlin Broadhead, "Trade and Politics on the Congo Coast, 1770–1870" (Ph.D. dissertation, Boston University, 1971), remains unpublished.

nities clustered around men who had grown rich on the newer forms of trade.[27]

The Ovimbundu kings, who had dominated the southern commercial system terminating at Benguela, extended their slaving frontier by the end of the eighteenth century to the headwaters of the Zambezi, where the trade spurred a proliferation of political titles and incipient centralization among the Luchazi. Ovimbundu lineage authorities responded quickly to the rising demand for wax and ivory and pioneered the formation of large armed caravans that ranged far to the east after 1850.[28] Caravans of this sort became the arbiters of politics in many parts of Equatorial Africa as the old kingdoms disintegrated, leaving political vacuums that the warlord-leaders of these mobile armies filled with ease, raiding villages, exacting tribute where they could find it, and trading where superior force necessitated. Caravan merchants frequently hired their men out as mercenaries in the service of local nobles fighting for political titles, thus contributing to the disintegration of several established political systems.

The Lunda *mwaant yaav* were major beneficiaries of the expanded slaving frontier between 1750 and 1850 but then fell as civil strife engendered by the presence of mercenary merchant caravans engulfed their kingdom. As Kasanje and Ovimbundu demands for slaves in the first half of the nineteenth century exceeded the Lunda kings' ability to meet them, subordinate western Lunda titleholders nurtured direct contacts with the traders from the west. Increased demands for wax and ivory after 1850 contributed to the changing political balance by converting the Cokwe, whose homeland contained abundant swarms of bees and herds of elephants, into formidable competitors. The Cokwe invested their commercial profits in women purchased from passing Ovimbundu and Imbangala caravans to produce a rapid increase in population. During the 1870s entire Cokwe villages began moving among the Lunda in search of new supplies of wax and wild rubber made from the sap of vines common in the southern savannas. The Cokwe expanded their ivory-hunting expeditions into large armed trading caravans that

[27] Joseph C. Miller, "Slaves, Slavers, and Social Change," in Franz-Wilhelm Heimer, ed., *Social Change in Angola* (Munich, 1973), 9–29.
[28] For the present, one must still consult Childs, *Umbundu Kinship and Character*, 190–215, for the nineteenth-century Ovimbundu.

32

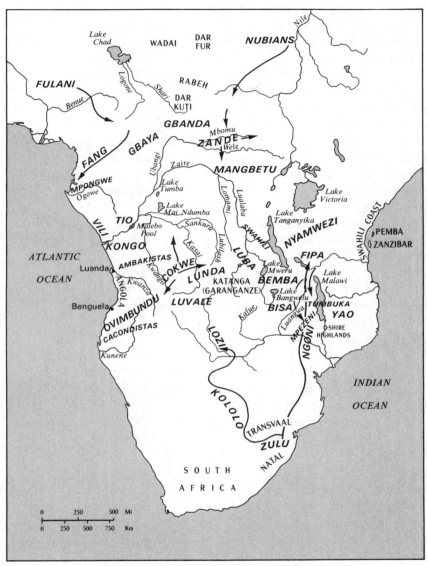

Central and Southern Africa: Nineteenth Century

joined Lunda nobles then fighting for the *mwaant yaav* title, plunging the Lunda empire into a cycle of civil wars that ended only with its total disintegration in the 1880s. The migrating Cokwe villages had in the meantime spread Cokwe linguistic and cultural traits throughout a large region on both sides of the Kasai.[29]

The shift from slave trading to legitimate commerce brought Portuguese Angola to the brink of bankruptcy, as the old slaving oligarchy fought futilely against their African neighbors' control over the new commodities. Officials in Luanda responded to the hard times during the 1840s and 1850s with ill-fated military expeditions along the borders of the area under Portuguese control, and Lisbon contributed a better coordinated series of government-sponsored explorations in the 1870s and 1880s. Portuguese culture diffused widely during this period. Its most effective bearers were not Portuguese but communities of African traders like the Vili or Zombo, so-called Ambakistas from near Luanda and Cacondistas from the southern Ovimbundu highlands. A new postal system and halting administrative reforms consolidated government authority in a few districts; merchants concentrated on devising methods to force Africans to transport the new exports to the coast. Commercial agriculture developed only sporadically, retarded by labor shortages and inadequate roads to convey the coffee, sugar, sisal, and manioc produced on plantations spreading northeast of Luanda and over the Ovimbundu highlands. Slavery was abolished in gradual stages, but planters continued to import slaves from the east under a variety of legal subterfuges and supplemented them with contract laborers recruited, usually by force, from within the colony's borders. In the areas of European settlement and agriculture the African population steadily lost their lands to planters and merchant creditors and moved from their own domains into new settlements centered around European plantations and small towns. This shift marked the beginning of the decline from relatively independent agricultural production to an impoverished dependence on the Portuguese and on the world economy that was later to characterize nearly all of Equatorial Africa.[30]

---

[29] Slightly out of date but still useful is Joseph C. Miller, "Cokwe Trade and Conquest," in Gray and Birmingham, eds., *Pre-Colonial African Trade*, 175–201.

[30] Douglas Wheeler and René Pélissier, *Angola* (London, 1971), 51–83. Still useful here, as elsewhere, is James Duffy, *Portuguese Africa* (Cambridge, Mass., 1961). Also see Jill R.

The nineteenth-century northern savannas suffered a surge in the depredations of Sudanic slavers searching for captives to sell in the markets of northern and western Africa. Fulani lords in the Cameroon grasslands joined the older Muslim sultanates of the central Sudan and new bands of Nubian traders from the upper Nile in sending armed caravans that so devastated parts of these regions that virtually no social or political institutions now survive from earlier centuries. Villages fleeing south swarmed into the valleys of the Ubangi and the Mbomu, settling in heterogeneous mixtures of peoples and pushing the Bantu linguistic frontier south to the fringes of the forest. Peoples from similarly diverse backgrounds established themselves as Gbaya along the headwaters of the Sangha and the Lobaye and others just north of them regrouped and became known as Gbanda. Lineages displaced from the upper Sangha moved southward in a drift of entire villages similar to the expansion of the Cokwe that carried them through the forest until they emerged as Fang on the Lower Ogowe around 1870. Many of the immigrant Fang became traders and began selling their ivory and rubber to Mpongwe from the Gabon; their dynamic and individualistic ethic put them in a strong position to profit from the later development of agricultural and extractive industries in Gabon.[31]

Muslim warlords settled in the wake of the slave raiders and founded a series of short-lived slave-trading sultanates among the lineages of the northern savannas. One of the largest and most durable, the sultanate of Dar Kuti, was located among the Gbanda living on the eastern sources of the Shari river. Nubian traders and raiders entered the eastern regions from the Nile Valley after 1855 and fought one another until one of them, Zubair, achieved supremacy in the 1860s. Zubair's ascendancy lasted only until the 1870s, when a former lieutenant, Rabeh, extended Nubian slave raiding toward the west and installed himself as an independent warlord in the lands between Zubair's domains and the sultanate of Dar Kuti. Rabeh's numerous mercenaries raided unchallenged from the upper Mbomu to Wadai in the 1880s and then moved

Dias, "Black Chiefs, White Traders, and Colonial Policy near the Kwanza: Kabuku Kambilo and the Portuguese, 1873-1896," *Journal of African History*, 17, 2 (1976):245-66.

[31] On the Fang, see Giles Sautter, *De l'Atlantique au Fleuve Congo* (2 vols) (Paris, 1966), 748 and sources cited.

north into the Sudan to mount a campaign against the kingdom of Bornu west of Lake Chad.[32] Through the rapid turnover among the savanna warlords, the Sudanic sultanates of Wadai and Dar Fur, the Fulani emirates, and others continued their pursuit of slaves in the northern savannas.

Only the savanna-dwellers living under the Bandia and Vungara warlords escaped the worst ravages of the Sudanic slavers. New small Zande states tended to form on the fringes of the existing cluster of Vungara kingdoms, thus spreading Zande culture farther to the east and south. In the west, three rather large Bandia states—Bangassou, Rafai, and Bondo—took shape in the nineteenth century and engaged in substantial slaving, selling captured men to the Nubians and keeping the women for redistribution to subordinate lords and to favored warriors. Mangbetu warlords just to the south employed techniques of conquest and assimilation similar to those of the Zande and developed a single kingdom under a noble called Nabiembali in the 1830s. Their commercial contacts led west down the rivers, where they traded palm oil, iron ore, and forest products with Bobangi merchants.

Eastern Equatorial Africa in the nineteenth century came increasingly under the influence of merchants and warlords connected with the Indian Ocean trading system of eastern Africa. By the beginning of the century individual east African traders in search of ivory, coastal Swahili as well as Nyamwezi and Yao from the highlands beyond the lakes, had penetrated as far west as the court of the Luapula *kazembe*, but the first phases of this commerce had primarily stimulated local trading systems. Non-noble Bisa merchants from east of Lake Bangwelu mounted ivory caravans very much like those of the Vili and Ovimbundu and probed the Luba lands north of the Luapula and west of Lake Tanganyika. Local Luba titleholders, especially those from one of the small western Luba states on the Lomami River, established a competing commercial system based on royal commercial agents and cooperative local authorities united by their common heritage of the *bulopwe* ideology. Political centralization in what was misnamed a Luba Lomami "empire" never extended far beyond its nuclear provinces in the far southwest. Elsewhere it remained a network of wealthy

[32] On the Nubian traders, see Richard Gray, *A History of the Southern Sudan, 1839–1889* (London, 1961), 20–69.

ivory monopolists who resembled contemporary merchant communities more than the kings whose political heritage they claimed.[33]

The eastern African slave trade, expanding like its Atlantic counterpart, penetrated Equatorial Africa after 1800 along a new trade route running from the Nyamwezi around the southern end of Lake Tanganyika toward the Luapula *kazembe*. Bemba from the headwaters of the Chambezi became active slave raiders under a powerful warlord elite headed by holders of a title known as the *chitimukulu*, one of the old Luba titles long present among Bemba lineages but never before centralized. By the 1850s they had become trading warlords typical of the era.[34] At about the same time, large Nyamwezi ivory and slave caravans weakened the Luapula *kazembe* by trading with their provincial lords. The leader of one of these caravans, Msiri, eventually gained full control of the entire western part of the kingdom, thereafter known as Katanga or Garanganze. Msiri's close relations with the east African traders kept him well supplied with guns, which he exchanged for the ivory, slaves, and copper available locally, and his warriors gave the Lunda more reliable protection from Swahili, Bemba, and other slave raiders than had the last of the weakened *kazembe*.[35]

Swahili caravans sent out by the sultan of Zanzibar in the 1860s had better luck among the Luba Lomami, where they established permanent armed camps very much like those of Zubair. The more successful of them shed all but the most nominal subordination to the Zanzibar sultan and founded independent camps that grew to comprise thousands of slave fieldhands cultivating extensive plantations, warriors and bearers who kept large warehouses filled with trade goods, and numerous other retainers living in populous towns along the Lualaba. Islam, the religion of the Swahili overlords, spread among the uprooted populations of the camps, and the Swahili language diffused as a second tongue spoken everywhere east of the Lubilash. Several major warlords divided the territory into fiefdoms in which they claimed monopolies over ivory trading and slave raiding, but their enormous armed caravans ranged as far north as the Zande sultanates and as far west as the Sankuru. They

[33] Anne Wilson, "Long Distance Trade and the Luba Lomami Empire," *Journal of African History*, 13, 4 (1972):575–90.
[34] Andrew Roberts, *A History of the Bemba* (Madison, 1974).
[35] Vansina, *Kingdoms of the Savanna*, 227–35.

coordinated their activities only minimally until the 1870s, when Hamed bin Muhammad, a Swahili born in Zanzibar and better known as Tippu Tib, imposed a rough-and-ready hegemony over all trade north and east of the Sankuru. Slave raiding for captives to sell to local authorities in exchange for ivory and other products as well as to recruit soldiers, bearers, and fieldhands, continued unabated even though British efforts to end slave exports on the east African coast gradually took effect after 1873.[36]

Immigrant warlords from southern Africa, leading mobile bands of cattle-herding warriors fleeing Shaka's Zulu regiments in Natal, crossed the Zambezi at several points around 1830, disrupting local kings and merchants from the Lozi kingdom in the far west to the shores of Lake Malawi in the east. A heterogeneous band of Sotho and Tswana peoples called Kololo entered a weakened Lozi kingdom during a prolonged succession dispute between its northern and southern factions. The Kololo king, Sebitwane, defeated the Lozi armies and drove the surviving Lozi royalty into the hills northeast of the floodplain. Sebitwane consolidated a strong kingdom by installing aristocratic Kololo warlords over the local farmers and fishermen, encouraging marriage between the Kololo and the Lozi, conceding places in the Kololo administrative structure to local village headmen, and incorporating their representatives in councils at the royal courts. These policies, like those of the Zande and Mangbetu, introduced profound Kololo influences in language, manners, and political institutions. But Sebitwane's death in 1851 opened latent rifts among the Kololo that led eventually to their defeat at the hands of Lozi royals who restored the ancient line of Lozi kings in 1865. The return of claimants to the ancient Lozi political titles no more resurrected the earlier Lozi political structures than had the use made of *bulopwe* ideology among the Luba Lomami. The postrestoration powers behind the Lozi throne seem to have been nonroyal ivory traders from the northern part of the kingdom led by an official known by his title of *ngambela*. Squabbling among the weak rival claimants to the kingship allowed the

---

[36] Tippu Tib's autobiography, *Maisha ya Hamed bin Muhammed el Murjebi yaani Tippu Tip* has been translated and edited by Wilfred Whiteley (Nairobi, 1966). Vansina, *Kingdoms of the Savanna*, 235–50, summarizes this period, but see also M. Crawford Young, "The Congo," in James Kritzeck and William H. Lewis, eds., *Islam in Africa* (New York, 1969), 250–69.

ngambela's faction to dominate Lozi politics until another noble, Lubosi, took power as king Lewanika in 1878.[37] Another Nguni warleader named Zwangendaba led his band of refugees across the middle Zambezi in 1835 and paused in the highlands between Lake Malawi and the Chambezi river where they became known as Ngoni. Zwangendaba's warriors assimilated large numbers of people from the populations through whose lands they passed and stole cattle to form a compact settlement several thousands strong. The dense mass of people and animals rapidly exhausted the capacity of the land to support them wherever they stopped, and so the ecological consequences of their successes forced them to move every three or four years, devastating the western part of the *undi* kingdom and adding numerous Chewa and Tumbuka before they left Equatorial Africa in 1843 or 1844 to settle in the cattle-rich country just to the northeast of Lake Malawi.

Zwangendaba's death in about 1848 split the band and several sections scattered to find permanent homes in the area between the Luangwa and Lake Malawi. The largest band settled just west of the lake under a warleader named Mbelwa and another, under the generalship of Mpenzeni, settled in the western marches of the *undi*'s kingdom. In the process they administered the death blow to the *undi*'s already faltering state and substituted new warlord regimes based on aristocracies of cattle-keeping Ngoni surrounded by local farmers grouped in large villages and growing crops to support their capitals. Settlement and intermarriage diluted the original Nguni culture of the intruders with strong infusions of local Malawi practices, but Nguni political and military institutions tended to survive.[38]

The widespread destruction occasioned by Ngoni passage and settlement coincided with intensified slave raiding from other quarters during the 1850s. The Yao, who had for some years traded peacefully for ivory to the west of Lake Malawi, began to send large slave-raiding parties that devastated parts of the Shire Highlands

[37] In addition to Gerald Caplan, *Elites of Barotseland, 1878–1969* (London, 1970), and Mainga, *Bulozi under the Luyana Kings*, for this period also see J. D. Omer-Cooper, *Zulu Aftermath* (Evanston, 1969), ch. 8: and John D. Flint, "Trade and Politics in Barotseland during the Kololo Period," *Journal of African History*, 11, 1 (1970):71–86.
[38] See Omer-Cooper, *Zulu Aftermath*, ch. 5, and Langworthy, *Zambia Before 1890*, ch. 14. Also see especially Thomas T. Spear, *Zwangendaba's Ngoni, 1821–1890: A Political and Social History of a Migration* (Madison, 1972).

south of the lake and penetrated as far west as the Luangwa, where they added to miseries brought by Bemba raiders.[39] Mercenary armies from the lower Zambezi, known as Chikunda, also swarmed into the area and contributed to the chaos that enveloped the local lineages that had managed to escape assimilation into one or another of the Ngoni states.[40]

From the perspective of Equatorial Africa, the European campaign against the Atlantic slave trade had contributed to intensified slave raiding everywhere except in the areas nearest the Atlantic. The pace of cultural change had quickened as Muslim war leaders from the Swahili coast and from the margins of the Sahara spread Islam in both the southern and northern savannas and as Portuguese culture diffused outward from Angola. Other demographic and cultural changes were under way as Swahili, Ngoni, Zande, and Mangbetu regrouped populations in new patterns and as Fang and Cokwe embarked on assimilative migrations extending over hundreds of miles. Political elites from the days of kings survived in a few places—among the Kongo, Tio, Ovimbundu, and Lunda—but they were uniformly on the defensive as wealthy but nonaristocratic traders threatened their authority. In Luba Lomami and among the Bemba and the Lozi new groups assumed power under the cover of ancient titles. An age of traders and warlords had dawned, but their states often proved unstable and rarely outlived their founders, as the fractious history of the Nubians, the eastern Zande, the Kololo and the Ngoni demonstrated. Those that survived into the 1880s found themselves faced with rival traders and warleaders from outside the continent who during the next four decades would follow their trade routes into the heart of the continent and would ultimately bring down the political and commercial structures they had erected.

European

The trends toward integration into the world economy and hardships inflicted on Equatorial African farmers by African warlords and merchants continued with the appearance of

---

[39] For the Yao, see Edward A. Alpers, *Ivory and Slaves in East Africa* (London, 1975), and earlier publications cited therein.
[40] On the Chikunda, see Allen F. Isaacman, "The Origin, Formation and Early History of the Chikunda of South Central Africa," *Journal of African History*, 13, 3 (1972):443–62.

European competitors on the region's commercial trails. Their advance occurred against a background of growing European technological sophistication, as medical discoveries—especially the use of quinine as an effective antimalarial drug and the drinking of boiled water to prevent dysentery—allowed natives of the world's temperate regions to withstand the diseases of tropical latitudes for the first time. Simultaneous improvements in transportation and communications put the vast resources of metropolitan governments, business corporations, and churches at the effective disposal of Europeans in Africa. European governments agreed to respect one another's exclusive access to various parts of the continent at a conference held in Berlin in 1884–85, but their diplomacy produced few changes in the rhythms of life in Equatorial Africa until after World War I. Metropolitan capitals generally left the missionaries, company agents, settlers, military men, and colonial officials on the scene free to act according to their own standards, and goals of the men on the spot turned out to differ remarkably little from those of the merchants and warlords who had preceded them. They prolonged the unrestrained scramble after Equatorial Africa's resources during this period, roughly 1880 to 1920, bringing all but the most remote villages into intimate contact with world markets and thus eliminating the last remnants of local autonomy that had survived the slow erosion of preceding centuries.

A rash of European explorers in Equatorial Africa—Livingstone, Stanley, and Savorgnan de Brazza, the best known among them—generated a crescendo of publicity that helped to bring European ministers to the Berlin Conference of 1884–85. The doctrine of "effective occupation" accepted at that meeting meant that veteran explorers and assorted missionaries already on the spot became crucial to each European nation's pretensions to sovereignty in Africa as they sought to meet the conditions of the treaty. De Brazza's travels between 1875 and 1884 up the Ogowe and behind the Loango coast gave France title to all of Equatorial Africa west and north of the Zaïre and Ubangi rivers. Stanley's descent of the Zaïre and subsequent activities south of the lower river, together with German-led expeditions into the lower Kasai helped Léopold II, king of the Belgians, to secure rights over the remainder of the Zaïre basin in the name of the International African Association, a thinly disguised front for an international consortium consisting of

41

Léopold and assorted financial backers. London ignored Portugal's claims to the entire savanna between Angola and Mozambique and permitted an activist consular official, Harry Hamilton Johnston, to proclaim a British protectorate in concert with Cecil Rhodes's aggressive British South Africa Company over British missionaries near Lake Malawi. The British South Africa Company asserted its own claims to mineral rights and exclusive jurisdiction everywhere else between the Zambezi and the Zaïre watershed, except in Lozi territories where the king Lewanika won a British protectorate that not only preserved the Lozi kingdom intact but also significantly strengthened the position of the king within it.[41]

Léopold's Congo Independent State, the administrative agency of the International African Association, set the pace and style for European occupation of Equatorial Africa with the extreme penuriousness of its administration, its aggressive quest for natural resources through reliance on unrestrained private concessionary companies, the often brutal exploitation of African labor, and an economy based on gathering and transporting wild produce—mainly ivory and wild rubber—without significant capital investment. But it operated under severe fiscal constraints owing to an expensive obligation to end the slave trade within the basin of the Zaïre without imposing tariffs on legitimate commerce. The Independent State launched steamboats to wrest control of the interior river trade from the Tio and Bobangi and constructed a railroad linking the coast to Malebo Pool. These enterprises expended so significant a portion of available State funds that Léopold lacked financial resources to intensify the exploitation of ivory and rubber in the interior. He therefore resorted to the awarding of substantial concessions to several private corporations modeled on Rhodes's British South Africa Company; those in the Independent State received commercial monopolies, mineral rights, local police power, and general administrative responsibilities as well as tax advantages. Where existing traders and warlords were powerful and efficient, Léopold simply recognized them as official agents of the Independent State, as he did in 1887 with his appointment of Tippu Tib as governor of Stanley Falls with responsibility over the entire Swahili-dominated area. The Belgian king retained so little

---

[41] Mainga, *Bulozi under the Luyana Kings*, 128–206, and Caplan, *Elites of Barotseland*, 1–73.

effective authority over the activities of the concessionaires that they enjoyed an autonomy close to that of the African merchants and warlords whose places they hoped to take.

During the early 1890s the Congo Independent State and its affiliated companies undertook a series of military expeditions aimed at forcing out competing merchants and warlords whom they could not dislodge by treaty. One expedition sought to incorporate Msiri's domains, but when it reached Shaba in 1891 it encountered a British South Africa Company representative anxious to secure mineral rights in the kingdom for the South Africans. In the ensuing confused negotiations, the Belgian officer in charge of Léopold's force shot Msiri and proclaimed Independent State authority over his domains. Subsequent armed columns broke the power of Cokwe caravans still roaming freely in the Lunda lands nearer the Kasai and helped restore a Lunda royal line near the center of the former empire. In the east relations between Léopold and his nominal governor, Tippu Tib, deteriorated as subordinate Swahili lords grew resentful of State competition for their ivory trade and attempts to limit their slave raiding. Tippu Tib's return to Zanzibar in 1891 freed them to engage in open hostilities, and from 1892 to 1895 Léopold's military forces drove most of the Swahili out of the Independent State.

European victories against existing warlords seldom altered significantly the lives of the villagers in the battle zones or elsewhere. Msiri's death and the suppression of Cokwe slave raiding in Shaba technically fulfilled the terms of the Berlin Conference but created no effective administration and left many Lunda lineages with more autonomy than they had known since the rise of kings centuries before. There were other continuities: state armies formally liberated thousands of Swahili slaves along the upper Lualaba but immediately enlisted them in Independent State service under conditions that, from their perspective, could hardly have differed from their former servitude.[42] In areas where administrative or diplomatic circumstances made incorporation of existing structures ex-

---

[42] For the early Congo Independent State, there are numerous authorities; one might begin with Ruth Slade, *King Leopold's Congo* (London, 1962). For a guide to recent work, see Bogumil Jewsiewicki, "Notes sur l'histoire socio-économique du Congo (1880–1960)," *Etudes d'histoire africaine*, 3 (1972):209–41.

pedient, Léopold's agents simply shored up tottering royal power, as in the Kuba kingdom and in certain Zande states.[43]

In French-claimed territories military commanders concluded treaties with most of the northern savanna warlords between 1887 and 1889 but hardly reduced their *de facto* autonomy. Later, armed columns raced toward Fashoda on the upper Nile in 1898, thus forcing a diplomatic showdown in Europe with the British and defeated Rabeh and the Sudanic sultanate of Wadai to end the worst of the slave raiding. The major short-term effect of these expeditions was to impose a severe strain on local populations forced to provide bearers and provisions for the French, draining manpower from the lineages no less than had the slave trading they prided themselves on having eliminated.

British occupation was less militaristic, with armed confrontations confined to the areas west and south of Lake Malawi where Harry Hamilton Johnston maneuvered his meager forces into a commanding position only by playing Yao, Swahili, Bemba, and Ngoni warlords against one another until by 1898 he had suppressed the slave trade and coerced the remaining powers into recognizing, however incongruously, the effective sovereignty of Britain's Nyasaland Protectorate.[44] The slave trade had ended, but hut taxes imposed by the protectorate and less indirect methods of labor recruiting produced a substitute stream of emigrants from the Nyasaland Protectorate and northeastern Northern Rhodesia who moved across the Zambezi to work on the farms of Southern Rhodesia and in the Transvaal gold mines. The British South Africa Company occupied Northern Rhodesia under the terms of a royal charter granted in 1894, but its effective presence was very uneven owing to the company's preoccupation with revolts and wars south of the Zambezi.[45] Missionaries stepped into the admin-

[43] For the Zande, Arlette Thuriaux-Hennebert, "Les grands chefs bandia et zande de la région Uele-Bomu (1860–1895)," *Etudes d'histoire africaine*, 3 (1972):167–207, and for the Kuba, Jan Vansina, "Du royaume kuba au 'Territoire des Bakuba'," *Etudes congolaises*, 12, 2 (1969):3–54.
[44] Standard is A. J. Wills, *An Introduction to the History of Central Africa* (3rd ed.; London, 1973), but this volume does not approach the viewpoint offered here. Two revisionist articles are Robin H. Palmer, "Johnston and Jameson: A Comparative Study in the Imposition of Colonial Rule," and B. S. Krishnamurthy, "Economic Policy, Land, and Labour in Nyasaland, 1890–1914," in Bridglal Pachai, ed., *The Early History of Malawi* (London, 1972), 293–322 and 384–404.
[45] For Northern Rhodesia at this period, although one must still begin with the outdated survey by L. H. Gann, *The Birth of a Plural Society* (Manchester, 1968), a forthcoming history

istrative void and sometimes became the only political authorities present after the elimination of the African political institutions.[46] Those attending Lewanika became little more than agents of their royal Lozi sponsor.

Nothing tempered the harshness of the private corporations' quest for ivory, rubber, and other exploitable wealth. Companies operating along the upper Zaïre and on the lower Kwango and Kasai demanded unrealistically high quotas of rubber while exercising little control over the methods their local agents employed to attain required levels of output. Abuses of the African populations subject to company control followed as company employees encouraged brutal punishment of African farmers unable to produce their alloted shares of rubber. Murders, the severing of hands and ears, and forced rubber gathering prevented the harvesting of adequate food and brought some areas to the brink of starvation until publicity emanating from British and American missionaries in the Kasai-Kwango region provoked international protests against the companies' ruthless methods and led to moderate reforms of the concession system in 1906. These and other pressures forced Léopold to cede the Congo Independent State to the Belgian government in 1908.[47] Inadequate financing and metropolitan supervision allowed a similarly harsh concessionary regime to dominate the French side of the Zaïre. Simultaneous administration demands for transportation and supplies prevented people in the most seriously afflicted regions from growing enough food to feed themselves. Concessionary companies eroded the authority left to remaining warlords in the northern savannas by the initial treaty arrangements, with company agents emerging everywhere as local despots in collaboration with local administrators. Very few missionaries were present in French Equatorial Africa to call attention to these abuses and many of them continued until after 1920.[48]

In Northern Rhodesia early twentieth-century mining and

by Andrew D. Roberts may be expected to fill a major gap in historical writing on Equatorial Africa.

[46] See Robert I. Rotberg, *Christian Missionaries and the Creation of Northern Rhodesia, 1880–1924* (Princeton, 1965).

[47] An extensive literature covers the Belgian assumption of responsibility for the Congo; the most recent publication in English is Stanley Shaloff, *Reform in Leopold's Congo* (Richmond, 1970).

[48] See the excellent and detailed study by Catherine Coquery-Vidrovitch, *Le Congo au Temps des Grandes Compagnies Concessionaires, 1898–1930* (Paris, 1972).

smelting technology did not allow profitable exploitation of the copper deposits of the Zaïre-Zambezi watershed. As a result many areas escaped the consequences of company rule manifested elsewhere in Equatorial Africa.[49] But the inhabitants of the Shire highlands of Malawi were displaced by European-owned cotton and tea plantations and forced to seek employment as laborers in the Europeans' fields. Low pay and harsh working conditions were typical there, as elsewhere, and European governments were uniformly unable and unwilling to regulate more than the worst excesses of the planters, commercial agents, and missionaries who settled in Equatorial Africa in this period.

On the whole the years from 1880 to 1920 were extremely difficult for most Equatorial Africans. Farmers suffered both the Muslim slave trade from northern and eastern Africa and the forced labor demanded by Europeans advancing from the south and west. African merchant communities lost their occupational niches as European firms established themselves along the coasts and gradually extended networks of small shops up the rivers and, as roads were built, into the interior. The depredations of the concessionary companies drove entire communities into remote and infertile regions. A disastrous fall in rubber prices and the exhaustion of rubber and ivory supplies after the turn of the century, coupled with the relatively costly transportation systems operated by the Europeans, meant that the export trade, which in African hands had helped to support many people for more than three centuries, entered a period of depression at the same time as Europeans were increasing people's dependence on it by destroying the last elements of autonomy left to local economies. The resulting malnutrition, combined with increased geographical mobility and the introduction of European diseases, produced a series of epidemics that swept through much of Equatorial Africa, producing local mortality rates of seventy and eighty percent.[50]

[49] For the early history of the Copperbelt, on the Northern Rhodesian side, see Richard Hall, *Zambia* (New York, 1965), 245–53.

[50] For the social and epidemiological history of the period, it is necessary to consult scattered references in the authorities cited. Terence O. Ranger, *The Agricultural History of Zambia* (Lusaka, 1971); Douglas Wheeler, "A Note on Smallpox in Angola, 1670–1875," *Studia*, 13–14 (1963):351–62; and Hermann Pössinger, "Interrelations between Economic and Social Change in Rural Africa: The Case of the Ovimbundu of Angola," in Heimer, ed., *Social Change in Angola*, 31–52, set a tone that promises to become prominent in a wide range of forthcoming studies.

Owing to the rudimentary development of European institutions during this period, the new colonies offered few opportunities for the African population. Mission stations, especially in the Kasai, west of Lake Malawi, and in parts of Angola, provided elementary literate education but could offer few jobs and often served as little more than refugee camps sheltering individuals fleeing disorders in the surrounding areas. The growth of towns—especially Brazzaville and Léopoldville on Malebo Pool, but also Luanda in Angola, Elizabethville in Katanga, and Stanleyville in northeastern Congo—stimulated African truck gardening and fishing enterprises to provision urban market places. The Union Minière du Haut Katanga (UMHK) began significant copper mining in Katanga after 1910 and thus provided some employment and limited opportunities for advancement. But economic stagnation was the rule for most Equatorial Africans, and those whom taxes and impoverishment forced into European employment generally migrated toward the better-developed economies south of the Zambezi rather than accept the strenuous and underpaid tasks of road building or service in colonial armies available nearer home.

The fundamental continuities linking the 1880–1920 period to the previous era of dominance by African merchants and warlords help to explain why "African resistance" to the extreme difficulties most people faced so rarely broke into violence. Open violence characterized relations between the two foreign elites, each supported by equally alien slave and mercenary armies, but local farmers offered only infrequent organized opposition to European penetration. The reasons for their apparent passivity lie in the economic hardships, malnutrition, sickness, and fragmentation of African social and political structures typical of the period. In addition, the still generally light yoke of direct administrative control in most regions and short-range opportunities as catechists or pastors and as soldiers and policemen in the areas of more intensive influence offered escape from the harshest features of existence. European rule in a form that people recognized as systematic or could differentiate from difficulties that had long beset them simply had not yet penetrated deeply into the fabric of African life. The few Equatorial African "revolts" that have received publicity in the literature of resistance—those of the Tetela in central Congo, the Angolan Ovimbundu in 1902, and John Chilembwe's 1915 uprising in Nyasa-

47

land—typically grew out of minorities that resorted to violence for reasons far more complex than opposition to European political overlordship.[51]

European merchants and warlords hardly brought colonial sovereignty to Equatorial Africa in the strict sense of coherent and penetrating administration by foreign governments. Most of them ravaged the land and the people beyond any control by their nominal superiors in Europe. Their main achievement was the exhaustion of natural resources exploitable without significant capital investment or sophisticated Western technology. Governments in Europe were only dimly aware of the starvation, disease, and the paralysis in African institutions that prevailed in Equatorial Africa. Tending to perceive these conditions through distorted racist lenses characteristic of the late nineteenth century, they did not suspect the extent to which they had contributed to the disasters they deplored. Their discovery after 1920 of the magnitude of the disorder coincided with a secular humanism rising in the aftermath of an idealistic European war and therefore generated a halting and often shortsighted desire to ameliorate the worst of these circumstances during the full colonial period that followed.

Technocratic Rule

Colonial Administrations

The full colonial period in Equatorial Africa began in the 1920s with the penetration of metropolitan bureaucratic institutions in colonies that had been acquired with reluctance or without adequate financing and then abandoned immediately to local interests unresponsive to direction from Europe. In the economic sphere, the colonial period brought recognition that the private companies' economy of pillage had bankrupted most of

[51] For the Tetela, see Thomas Turner, "Mouvements de résistance chez les Mongo du Sankuru," *Revue Congolaise des Sciences Humaines,* 2 (1971):59–84. On the Ovimbundu, see Douglas C. Wheeler and C. Diane Christensen, "To Rise with One Mind: The Bailundo War of 1902," in Heimer, ed., *Social Change in Angola,* 53–92, and Fola Soremekun, "The Bailundo Revolt, 1902," *African Social Research,* 16 (1973):449–73. There is a substantial literature on the Chilembwe revolt; the basic account is George Shepperson and Thomas Price, *Independent African* (Edinburgh, 1958). See also Robert I. Rotberg, "Psychological Stress and the Question of Identity: Chilembwe's Revolt Reconsidered," in Robert I. Rotberg and Ali A. Mazrui, eds., *Protest and Power in Black Africa* (New York, 1970), 337–73, and Ian and Jane Linden, "John Chilembwe and the New Jerusalem," *Journal of African History,* 12, 4 (1971):629–51.

the colonies and that the fiscal sulf-sufficiency demanded of African dependencies would require planned economic development touching the African population in new ways. With regard to the "native problem," as colonial powers tended to conceive of the presence of Equatorial Africans, most responded in terms of misguided efforts to "civilize" colonial populations through religious exhortation, forced labor, and limited instruction in reading and writing. The underlying tension between metropolitan planners and settler communities in Africa continued, surfacing most significantly when local Europeans rejected even the small numbers of schooled Christian Africans who desired acceptance as their social and political equals.

The Congo once again set an example followed by the other colonies of Equatorial Africa in its administration's determination to avoid deficits in the state budget. Restrictions on import duties inherited from the Berlin Treaty and the Independent State and Belgian unwillingness to commit metropolitan funds to the Congo left the colony enmeshed in a Léopoldian network of interlocking private corporations, mostly mining and transportation subsidiaries of the giant Société Générale. Huileries du Congo Belge (HCB), a Leverhulme subsidiary, and other agribusiness firms developed extensive palm and rubber plantations in the central portions of the colony. But much of the solution to persistent fiscal difficulties lay in passing as much of the financial burden as possible on to the African population through a capitation tax and obligatory and unpaid labor services to the state of sixty days or more each year.

The policy most damaging to rural Congolese was the compulsory cultivation of cash crops, implemented most extensively in cotton-growing regions in the northern savannas and in former Swahili areas along the Lualaba and in the oil palm areas of the Kasai. Forced cultivation yielded very little cash income to the average farmer, however, as monopsonist firms (HCB, Cotonco, and others) purchased African harvests at artificially low prices. The lack of economic incentive restricted output, but the administration misdirected its efforts to expand production into collective farming projects known as *paysannats*, intended to combine the expertise of African farmers with Western technology. The *paysannats* failed to increase output, damaged the delicate ecological

49

Equatorial Africa: Colonial and Independent

balance achieved by African farmers, and incurred the determined hostility of the Congolese who were forced to participate. The net effects of Belgian agricultural policies in the Congo were to instill a deep-seated mistrust of any centralized government and to preserve the rural poverty created during the worst years of rule by warlords and merchants.[52]

[52] The most comprehensive, though still limited, work on the Belgian Congo in English is Roger Anstey, *King Leopold's Legacy: The Congo under Belgian Rule, 1908–1960* (London, 1966).

Only a few of the French Equatorial African concessionary companies survived into the 1920s, but in the continued absence of government investment the remaining firms secured strong positions in transport, commerce, and the exploitation of the French colonies' natural resources. Small settler communities formed around these firms in the main towns of the federated colonies of the Afrique Equatoriale Française (AEF)—Libreville, the capital of Gabon; Pointe Noire, capital of Moyen Congo; Bangui, capital of Oubangui-Chari; and Brazzaville, capital of the Federation.[53] Local administrators customarily worked closely with the private interests to transfer the costs of colonial rule to the rural Africans while denying them significant benefits. Industry remained exclusively in European hands—gold and diamond mines in Oubangui-Chari, copper mines in Gabon and Moyen Congo, and logging of *okume*, a tree plentiful in the forests of Gabon and used in the manufacture of plywood. French planters cultivated coffee in Oubangui-Chari but denied African farmers entry into this relatively profitable market; instead Africans were subjected to a compulsory cotton cultivation regime similar to that of the Belgian Congo in the disadvantageous conditions it imposed. Moyen Congo proved to be one of the most impoverished territories of Equatorial Africa except in the environs of Brazzaville where Kongo developed small-scale commercial gardening. In an exceptional case of African prosperity, Fang in the northwestern Gabon region known as the Woleu-Ntem developed profitable cocoa farms. Both Kongo and Fang achieved their economic successes by modifying indigenous economic and social institutions, demonstrating the extent to which the rural poverty prevalent nearly everywhere else resulted from artificial economic arrangements that worked to the exclusive benefit of European companies and colonial governments.[54]

The full colonial period in Angola technically dated from new legislation promulgated by the Portuguese Republic declared in

On this, as for other aspects of the Belgian period, see Jewsiewicki, "Notes sur l'histoire". For political economy, see Michael Merlier, *Le Congo de la colonisation belge à l'independance* (Paris, 1962).

[53] The Afrique Equatoriale Française also included the colony of Tchad north of Oubangui-Chari; its history has not been included here with that of Equatorial Africa.

[54] One might consult Georges Balandier, *The Sociology of Black Africa*, tr. Douglas Garman (New York, 1970), for an insight into French attitudes toward development and its effects on the Kongo and the Fang. Jean Suret-Canale, *French Colonialism in Tropical Africa, 1900–1945*, tr. Till Gottheimer (New York, 1971), remains the most comprehensive treatment.

1910 and by Lisbon dictator Salazar's *estado novo* ("new state") after 1926, but existing patterns of rural exploitation continued in practice rather than yielding to the centralization typical elsewhere. The area under effective Portuguese control expanded eastward along the railroad constructed during the 1920s from Benguela to the Copperbelt, but the contemporaneous initiation of open-pit diamond mining near the Congo border brought Luanda no authority over the concessionary company responsible (DIAMANG) and few revenues. Large regions in the southeast and pockets of territory elsewhere remained economically unintegrated and all but beyond the weak administrative reach of the Angolan government. The essence of Portuguese colonial rule, from the point of view of most rural Africans, was forced labor and subjugation to an alliance of local planters, petty administrators, and bush traders, often members of related families resident in some areas for many decades. Head taxes, forced planting of cash crops saleable only at discriminatory prices (especially in the former Kasanje and Jinga areas along the middle Kwango), and arbitrary requisitions of labor for private plantations as well as for government road work were common in the administered areas. The presence of Portuguese settlers excluded Africans from gardening and fishing opportunities open to them elsewhere and drove Africans from their lands in colonized regions east of Luanda and in the Ovimbundu highlands. The little cash left in the hands of rural Angolans after payment of taxes often went to satisfy debts owed bush traders who customarily advanced the food and other necessities that farmers subjected to forced labor and cash cropping could not produce for themselves.[55]

British Central Africa, as the colonies of Nyasaland and Northern Rhodesia, together with Southern Rhodesia, became known informally after the termination of the British South Africa Company charter in 1924, experienced very uneven economic development. Improved mining technology made the Rhodesian copper deposits profitable during the 1920s and created a mining boom that led to the investment of hundreds of millions of dollars by the

[55] See Duffy, *Portuguese Africa*, 245-342, and Wheeler and Pélissier, *Angola*, 109-55. Michael Samuelson, *Education in Angola, 1878-1914* (New York, 1970), discusses the attitudes of the Portuguese Republic. The essays in Heimer, ed., *Social Change in Angola*, and in Ronald H. Chilcote, ed., *Protest and Resistance in Brazil and Angola* (Berkeley, 1972), provide recent viewpoints.

American-dominated Rhodesian Selection Trust and the South African–U.S.-backed Anglo-American Corporation. But prosperity on the Copperbelt stimulated no significant development in the surrounding African areas owing to its enclosure in a classic "enclave economy;" production was oriented exclusively toward foreign markets, few supplies were bought locally, low taxes were paid to the colonial government and low wages to local labor, and profits were either exported to overseas investors or reinvested locally within the enclave where they made no contribution to the general welfare.[56]

Vast areas of Northern Rhodesia, especially the Barotseland Protectorate (formerly Loziland) in the far west and Bemba districts in the northeast, remained untouched by the wealth concentrated on the Copperbelt and experienced disruptions in their carefully balanced agricultural systems as migrant laborers flocked to the mine compounds. European settlers in the highlands of southern Nyasaland displaced up to half the African farmers from their lands in some areas and reduced others to the status of squatters on white-owned estates. European farmers claimed the choicest lands along the railroad linking the Copperbelt to Southern Rhodesia and South Africa. Only the Tonga, who lived near the rail line, drew significant advantages from the colonial economy by selling maize to feed miners and Europeans living on the Copperbelt. Elsewhere planters successfully expelled Africans from unused land, extracted illegal rents, or employed discriminatory pricing to discourage Africans from cash crop cultivation.[57]

Administrative practices added significantly to the burdens suffered by rural Africans after 1920. In Angola, the tenuousness of effective central control allowed local officials to behave in arbitrary and often cruel fashion, as the fame of the *ciboko*, or hippopotamous-hide whip, testified. In theory Angolans were subject to an elaborate code called the *indigenato* designed to teach the virtues of Portuguese Catholic civilization; in practice the *indigenato*

[56] See Robert E. Baldwin, *Economic Development and Export Growth: A Study of Northern Rhodesia, 1920–1960* (Berkeley, 1966).

[57] See Ranger, *Agricultural History of Zambia*, and studies conducted by anthropologists at the Rhodes-Livingstone Institute. For Nyasaland, Bridglal Pachai, "Land Policies in Malawi: An Examination of the Colonial Legacy," *Journal of African History*, 14, 4 (1973):681–98, and H. Leroy Vail, "The Making of an Imperial Slum: Nyasaland and its Railways, 1895–1935," *Journal of African History*, 16, 1 (1975):89–112.

amounted to a justification for taxes and forced labor. Africans in the AEF were subject to a system of administrative justice called the *indigenat* that allowed local administrators effectively unlimited powers to fine, imprison, administer corporeal punishment, or subject to labor penalties any African who incurred their anger.

Belgian and British "native" policies contrasted with the "civilizing" intent of the Portuguese and French in the attention they devoted to the creation of superficially authentic African administrative structures. But in fact most of these reflected gross European misconceptions about the rural milieux. The Belgians developed an elaborate system of *chefferies* (chiefdoms) that would function as the lowest levels in the colonial bureaucracy; equivalent institutions in British Central Africa were termed Native Authorities. The unviability of institutions reflecting inaccurate European perceptions of conditions thirty to sixty years earlier doomed the entire effort to failure and contributed to the dissatisfaction of rural populations.

Rural Africans responded to economic oppression, administrative ineptitude, and personal cruelty in the rural areas first by trying to leave and secondly by resorting to violence in a few extreme instances. Flight took a variety of forms, most of them temporary and ineffective. School systems providing advanced instruction in Western manners, Christianity, and literacy offered one way out of rural poverty by training people for employment in the institutions of colonial rule—as pastors and catechists for the missions, as clerks and machinery operators for private business and government, and as teachers. Fully educated Africans had begun to graduate from mission schools in the western Congo, Angola, and Nyasaland even before the First World War, and significant numbers of them were presenting themselves for the few positions open during the 1920s. Nearly all hoped to rise to positions of power and respect within the colonial system, but they almost uniformly encountered rude rebuffs from local settler communities' racial prejudices, Protestant-Catholic rivalries, and competition with Europeans. Advanced education was in any case available only to a tiny minority of rural Africans; French and Portuguese indifference limited the numbers of schools in their colonies, and the restriction of instruction to only the most elementary levels was responsible in the Congo. The relatively extensive early development of educational facilities in Nyasaland failed to continue after British government policy shifted in the 1930s to emphasize vocational and agricultural training rather than the literate skills that offered escape from rural hardships.

A second means of escape from the rural areas was to move permanently or temporarily into the towns and industrial centers. Migrant labor became common as younger men left villages devoid of economic opportunity and dominated by their elders to seek higher incomes as unskilled laborers on European-owned plantations and in the mines of southern as well as Equatorial Africa. But mine owners and government officials regarded Africans as incapable of permanent urban settlement and devised labor contracts and pass systems to limit each individual's move to the town to a temporary stay. The main exceptions to the tendency to force Africans to remain in the rural areas occurred in the highly paternalistic "labor stabilization" policies adopted by the UMHK in Katanga. Migrant labor and flight to the swelling "native quarters" of Equatorial African towns rarely offered more than a temporary and unsatisfactory solution to the problems of rural poverty.

Most Africans endured the afflictions of colonial rule by remaining in the rural areas and making the best of the small opportunities available locally—elders defended minor forms of authority from assault by their juniors, small lineages maneuvered to gain control of government positions controlled by more powerful neighbors, fishermen dried fish for sale in the provincial towns, and so on.[58] The creative initiatives seized by Africans even under the constraints of colonial rule have received little emphasis from historians, but the intra-African dimensions of village politics, when they become known, will undoubtedly illuminate phenomena presently seen in simplistic terms of black-white relations. Semi-Christian and indigenous religious movements swept through parts of Equatorial Africa, but they were as much manifestations of processes of social and intellectual change present for as long as the historical record reveals as specific responses to colonial rule. The most famous were the Watch Tower or Kitawala in Nyasaland,

[58] Studies that have begun to satisfy the pressing need for local analyses are Jan Vansina, "Les Kuba et l'administration territoriale, 1919–1960," *Cultures et développement*, 4, 2 (1972):275–325, Vansina, *Tio Kingdom*, ch. 17, and Edouard Bustin, *Lunda under Belgian Rule: The Politics of Ethnicity* (Cambridge, Mass., 1975). One may also consult Wyatt MacGaffey, *Custom and Government in the Lower Congo* (Berkeley, 1970), and Colin Turnbull, *The Lonely African* (New York, 1962).

Northern Rhodesia, and eastern Congo, *muchapi* in Nyasaland in 1934, and the Church of Jesus Christ on Earth founded by Simon Kimbangu among the Kongo; many were led by marginally schooled younger men unable to find the places to which they aspired in the European bureaucracies.[59] Organized rural violence was uncommon. The most extensive outbreaks occurred in the late 1920s among the Gbaya of western Oubangui-Chari in an area that had never experienced the full force of French colonial rule, and among the Pende of the Kasai in 1931. The Pende "rebellion" resulted from a complex mixture of abuses by the HCB, falling world prices for palm oil, rivalries among the Pende, and over-reaction by nervous local officials who ordered an attack by Congo government troops.[60]

The increasing influence of metropolitan policymakers over affairs in Equatorial Africa had its most significant long-range effects in decisions taken after World War II to hand over most colonial government machinery to African bureaucrats and politicians. Unlike West Africa, where political evolution was in good part a direct response to pressures from nationalist-organized African masses, the origins of the final move toward independence in Equatorial Africa owed relatively little to widespread African group pressure. The educated Christian graduates of European schools had organized themselves in Native Associations in Nyasaland since before the First World War and in Northern Rhodesia beginning in the 1930s.[61] Congolese *évolués*, as the small group of educated men there were known, formed apolitical alumni associations connected with

[59] J. R. Hooker, "Witnesses and Watchtower in the Rhodesias and Nyasaland," *Journal of African History*, 6, 1 (1965):91–106; Terence O. Ranger, "Mchape: A Study in Diffusion and Interpretation," in Terence O. Ranger and Sholto Cross, eds., *The Problem of Evil in Eastern Africa, 1870–1970* (forthcoming); Ephriam Andersson, *Messianic Popular Movements in the Lower Congo* (Uppsala, 1958). For a case study embodying the view adopted here, see Jan Vansina, "Les mouvements religieux kuba (Kasai) à l'époque coloniale," *Etudes d'histoire africaine*, 2 (1971):155–87. Perhaps the most penetrating analysis is John M. Janzen and Wyatt Mac-Gaffey, *An Anthology of Kongo Religion* (Lawrence, 1974), 1–27.

[60] Faustin Mulambu-Mbuluya, "La révolte des Bapende (mai-septembre 1931)," *Congo-Afrique*, 11 (no. 52) (1971):115–36.

[61] For early African political activities in British Central Africa, see Robert I. Rotberg, *The Rise of Nationalism in Central Africa* (Cambridge, Mass., 1965); Roger Tangri, "Colonial and Settler Pressures and the African Move to the Politics of Representation and Union in Nyasaland," *Journal of African History*, 13, 2 (1972):291–304; and Ian Henderson, "The Origins of Nationalism in East and Central Africa: The Zambian Case," *Journal of African History*, 11, 4 (1970):591–603, and "Wage-Earners and Political Protest in Colonial Africa," *African Affairs*, 72 (no. 288) (1973):288–99. On the *évolués*, see Roger Anstey, "Belgian Rule in the Congo and the Aspirations of the 'Evolué' Class," in Lewis Gann and Peter Duignan, eds., *Colonialism in Africa* (London, 1969), 2:194–225.

56

the various mission school systems. In Luanda, educated Africans and mulattoes had organized study and cultural groups since the late nineteenth century. Although driven underground by the *estado novo* during the 1920s, many of them continued to meet clandestinely. But nowhere did the concerns of these men extend far beyond their personal problems of fighting discrimination or take account of the needs of rural Africans. Peasant farmers and migrant laborers remained unorganized, with the significant exception of the miners on the Rhodesian Copperbelt who formed trade unions in the 1930s and pioneered the use of confrontation tactics in Northern Rhodesia. The major instance before the late 1950s in which educated Africans mobilized the latent discontent in the countryside and the urban slums for political purposes occurred in Moyen Congo when André Matswa, an educated Kongo living in Paris, founded an *amicale* (or "friendly society") that was transferred back to Brazzaville in 1926; there unemployed school leavers synthesized it with Kongo and Kimbanguist ideas to generate a widespread anti-French protest. But the Amicalist movement was premature and led only to Matswa's imprisonment, government repression of its adherents, and a sullen withdrawal by many Kongo from any participation in government-sponsored programs, including the first elections held in the AEF after World War II.

The movement toward independence in Equatorial Africa gathered momentum in the French and British colonies when the ideas of post-World War II West African nationalism began to penetrate the circles of educated Africans there and to influence metropolitan policy. The postwar Fourth French Republic, partly in gratitude for the Free French alignment of the black Guayanese wartime AEF governor-general, Felix Eboué, extended political reforms to its Equatorial African possessions gradually in the 1940s and 1950s.[62] Local settlers, whose Vichy sympathies had influenced Eboué's decision to support the Free French, generally opposed the liberal currents in metropolitan thinking but were eventually overwhelmed, and their more enlightened elements began to seek alliances with moderate African politicians as means of protecting their economic positions during the transition toward what could by then be seen as inevitable political independence.

After intricate maneuvering between affiliated metropolitan po-

[62] See the biography by Brian Weinstein, *Eboué* (New York, 1972).

litical parties, factions within the settler communities, rivalries among competing African politicians, and attempts to mobilize rural farmers and urban populations, the former colonies of French Equatorial Africa became self-governing members of the French Communauté in 1958; Oubangui-Chari renamed itself the Central African Republic (CAR), and Moyen Congo became the Congo Republic. In the CAR, Bartholemé Boganda, an ordained Catholic priest, combined overwhelming support among the farmers of his country with minority settler cooperation to win elections but he encountered opposition from the majority of local French who controlled his country's economy, and died in a mysterious airplane crash on Easter 1959. Moyen Congo politics turned on the loyalties of three groups of urban immigrants—those from the impoverished northern parts of the country (Mbochi), the Kongo (or Laali) around Brazzaville, and the western Kongo (Vili) near the port of Point Noire. The Abbé Fulbert Youlou gained a slim parliamentary majority by bringing the Laali Amicalists to the polls for the first time in his support; his open willingness to cooperate with the French business community assured him of acceptance in those circles. African politics in Gabon centered on Mpongwe and Fang factions in Libreville; both sides were associated with French commercial and industrial interests in the colony, as well as with mission establishments, and the eventual winner, Léon Mba, posed no threat to continued close association between Gabon and France.[63] Self-government did not alter the fact that the major economic assets of the three new nations remained in the hands of expatriate French and that their governments were fundamentally dependent on French government aid for their most basic operations. Little could be done in any case for the rural citizens who had voted their new leaders into office in the false hope of an early end to the impoverishment of colonial rule.

The presence of strong European mining, planting, and commercial interests in Nyasaland and Northern Rhodesia deflected political development in those two colonies into a temporary amalgamation with the white-dominated southern parts of the continent. Settler and company fears of the introduction of "West Afri-

63 Historical studies of political evolution of the AEF are still wanting, but see John A. Ballard, "Four Equatorial States," in Gwendolyn M. Carter, ed., *National Unity and Regionalism in Eight African States* (Ithaca, 1966), 231–335; and Brian Weinstein, *Gabon: Nation-Building on the Ogooue* (Cambridge, 1966) for post-independence studies by political scientists.

can nationalism" into British Central Africa overcame their wariness of domination by the much stronger economies of Southern Rhodesia and South Africa, leading to formation of a white-controlled Federation of Rhodesia and Nyasaland (or Central African Federation) in 1953. African and Colonial Office recognition that federation would entrench southern African racialism in Equatorial Africa gave a spur to African political organization, as the leaders of the local Native Associations combined into the Nyasaland National Congress (NNC) and the Northern Rhodesia African National Congress (NRANC). But these early pressure groups failed to arouse enthusiasm among the mineworkers of the Copperbelt or among Nyasaland plantation workers and migrant laborers.

The Federation soon began to break apart over the Colonial Office's intermittent defense of African rights and over increasing evidence of Southern Rhodesian prosperity at the expense of its two northern partners. The tide turned toward eventual independence in 1958–59 as two of the younger and more radical Nyasaland politicians, H. B. M. Chipembere and Kanyama Chiume, invited a Nyasaland physician then residing in Ghana, Dr. Hastings Kamuzu Banda, to lead a reformed Nyasaland African National Congress (NANC) and as more assertive Northern Rhodesian politicians under the leadership of Kenneth Kaunda formed the Zambia African National Congress (ZANC). Banda's charisma brought rural Nyasalanders into politics for the first time in widespread civil disturbances, while the ZANC applied itself to drawing the Copperbelt mineworkers and the neglected farmers of Northern Rhodesia into the battle. Federal officials reacted to these challenges by jailing the new leadership, thus converting Banda, Kaunda, and others into martyrs in the eyes of their followers and dooming the Federation to an early end.[64]

Political developments in the French and British colonies of Equatorial Africa affected the Congo only belatedly and Angola hardly at all before 1960. Responsible Belgian officials as late as 1956 foresaw virtually no possibility of political change in the Congo, but in 1958 and 1959 a few Congolese évolués introduced West African nationalist ideas in Léopoldville circles. Simultane-

[64] For the Federation, see Patrick Keatley, *The Politics of Partnership* (Baltimore, 1963); for nationalism, David C. Mulford, *Zambia, The Politics of Independence, 1957–1964* (New York, 1968), and Philip Short, *Banda* (Boston, 1974).

ously urban riots and rural unrest revealed to dismayed Belgian officials that they had lost control of events in the colony. They began hasty negotiations with Congolese leaders, who at the same time embarked on whirlwind political campaigns to channel the seething rural discontent, and accelerated a half thought-out timetable for independence that in the end would move faster than either side was prepared to control.[65] In Angola the Portuguese strengthened their military and police forces, while dissident Africans either fled into exile or intensified their secret plotting in Luanda and other cities.[66] But neither negotiation nor repression would prove capable of containing the volatile mixture of nationalist ideology and rural discontent present in these colonies.

The foregoing sketch neglects important themes particular to French, British, Portuguese, and Belgian colonialism and to the internal development of the individual colonies between 1920 and 1959 in favor of elaborating the broader patterns of change that generated mines and miners, settler communities, rapidly growing towns filled with unemployed men, and literate African elites out of the essentially rural Africa of 1920. It rests on the fact that the vast majority of Equatorial Africans even in 1959 remained farmers and temporary residents of towns. It should be clear that, in addition to the significant tensions between Africans and Europeans present under colonialism, there were also important divisions among the components of what has sometimes erroneously been termed the "colonial monolith" and that many kinds of intra-African rivalries lay beneath the larger communal conflicts associated with "tribalism." The colonial period did not leave the African population helplessly immobilized except for occasional violent outbursts of "resistance" but introduced extremely adverse conditions under which Africans made the best of a bad situation in a variety of ways only now becoming visible to scholars.

Nationalist interlude

Nationalist leadership in Equatorial Africa triumphed between 1959 and about 1965, but most of the regimes of that period proved to be short-lived and solved none of the per-

---

[65] M. Crawford Young, *Politics in the Congo* (Princeton, 1965), and Jean-Claude Willame, *Patrimonialism and Political Change in the Congo* (Stanford, 1972), among others.

[66] See John Marcum, *The Angolan Revolution: The Anatomy of an Explosion (1950–1962)* (Cambridge, 1969), and Basil Davidson, *In the Eye of the Storm* (London, 1972), 145–82.

sistent problems inherited from the colonial period—rural poverty, dependence on foreign economies, and unfulfilled desires for education and material wealth that would earn the respect of a Eurocentric world. After 1965 country after country replaced Western-style representative institutions with authoritarian forms of government, civilian or military, similar in form if not in rhetoric to the administrative rule that had characterized the colonial period. Leaders of the independent nations tended to accept their seemingly inescapable clientage to European economies but in so doing risked the hostility of urban mobs and peasant jacqueries resentful of apparent government neglect of their problems. Angola, still a Portuguese colony, belatedly entered a phase of administrative centralization and penetration of the rural areas similar to developments in the remainder of Equatorial Africa after the 1920s. At the same time African liberation movements initiated anti-Portuguese guerilla warfare and began their own programs of social and economic reconstruction in the northwestern and southeastern corners of the territory. As of the early 1970s it could be seen that the continuities linking the period before 1960 to the era of political autonomy still outnumbered the beginnings of change brought by independence.

The price of independence in Equatorial Africa, as everywhere in Africa, had been a legacy of European parliamentary institutions based on mass political participation. Elections, parties, and a clear constitutional distinction between the legislative, judicial, and executive branches of the new governments functioned in the hands of nationalist elites until about 1965 in most countries but then ran afoul of unruly urban mobs, disgruntled workers, peasants in revolt against any form of centralized authority, and bureaucrats and politicians who indulged in an ostentatious style of living that reflected their aspirations for "European" respectability but contrasted too sharply with the continued poverty of the majority of the population. The constitutions bestowed at independence uniformly proved inappropriate to handle the conditions confronting governments in Africa.

The Belgian Congo became fully independent as the Congo (Léopoldville) in 1960 and immediately disintegrated as tensions concealed beneath the veneer of Belgian administration surfaced in the form of army mutiny, secession of the country's richest provinces, and rural rebellion. Popular discontent during 1959 had raced far ahead of Belgian officials and Congolese politicians alike and outdistanced the final round of parliamentary elections and political maneuvering in early 1960. A government headed by Patrice Lumumba took office in Léopoldville as a result of an unstable compromise between Lumumba's party, the Mouvement National Congolais-Lumumba (MNC-L), and the Kongo leader who controlled the restive citizenry of Léopoldville and the recalcitrant rural populace in the surrounding area. These were the people who in 1959 had provoked Belgium's hasty departure and they still retained the key to effective government from the country's capital. Lumumba's political style, reminiscent of radical West African nationalism, had been effective in aggregating several local minorities into a superficially Pan-Congo coalition[67] but had alarmed both the Belgians and the directors of the European corporations on the Copperbelt. Lumumba was therefore vulnerable when the volatility of the Congolese majority first manifested itself in the form of an army mutiny, followed by administrative breakdown in the rural areas. Sporadic violence erupted in provincial towns, and Moise Tshombe, the top Katanga politician and a man with acknowledged close connections to European business circles on the Copperbelt, took advantage of the growing paralysis in Léopoldville to declare his province an independent state.

The disintegration of the Congo dealt a death blow to the Belgian-style constitution with which the country had begun its existence, although politicians limped through five more years of intermittent constitutional governments until a military strongman, General Joseph Mobutu, took power in 1965. Lumumba died an apparent victim of assassination after he had summoned United Nations troops to end the Katanga secession but then, fearing the unresponsiveness of the UN command to Léopoldville's directives, requested additional unilateral assistance from the Soviet Union; unknown enemies kidnapped him to avoid what they perceived as the opening of the Congo to "communist influence." The United Nations armed forces returned Katanga to the Congo government in early 1963, but their subsequent departure left a power vacuum in the unadministered rural portions of the country, allowing popu-

[67] Thomas Turner, "Congo-Kinshasa," in Victor Olorunsola, ed., *The Politics of Cultural Sub-Nationalism in Africa* (Garden City, 1972), 195–283.

lar discontent to surface once more in the form of uprisings among the Pende, in northern Katanga, around Stanleyville, and in the former Swahili areas in eastern Congo.[68] The central Congo government in Kinshasa (the renamed capital, formerly Léopoldville) responded to the prospect of renewed disintegration by again calling for outside aid, this time to Tshombe who took office as president and deployed former Katangan troops and bands of white mercenaries who suppressed the rural rebellions by 1965. Victorious militarily, Tshombe suffered politically from his continued close identification with former colonial powers, and his government fell after a parliamentary impasse that was resolved only when General Mobutu, backed by a reformed national army, dissolved the country's representative institutions and assumed power in the first step of the Congo's return to administrative rule.[69]

The three Equatorial African members of the French Communauté temporarily preserved their parliamentary institutions but did so at the expense of virtual surrender to local and metropolitan French business interests; eventually they, too, moved toward authoritarianism. President Mba in Gabon had assumed power with the open backing of French and other foreign financial interests, whose timber, iron, manganese, and other industries made his country one of the wealthiest in Equatorial Africa and employed or otherwise influenced most of Gabon's politically active population. Socialist-oriented youths, trade unionists, and others unconnected with Mba's regime or with its backers, used the country's Paris-inspired democratic political institutions to mount vociferous opposition to what they termed their president's "neocolonialist" orientation. The resulting parliamentary confrontation provoked an army mutiny that expelled Mba in 1964 in a pattern that was to become familiar elsewhere, but in this case the French rescued Mba and restored the country's nominally representative institutions. Mba, back in power under French tutelage but vulnerable to his political opponents, could ill afford an overt move toward authoritarianism and so tolerated a smoldering opposition

---

[68] Benoit Verhaegen, *Rébellions au Congo* (Bruxelles, 1966?), vols. 1 and 2, for exhaustive studies. Also see M. Crawford Young, "Rebellion and the Congo," in Rotberg and Mazrui, eds., *Protest and Power in Black Africa*, 968–1011.

[69] This and the following accounts of recent events have been compiled from a variety of often conflicting and incomplete journalistic accounts, except where more scholarly studies are noted. The large number of unknowns remaining render the analysis far from definitive.

until 1967, when he declared a one-party state and suspended the national assembly. His death from natural causes late in the same year terminated the career of one of Equatorial Africa's more durable strongmen.

David Dacko, Boganda's successor in the Central African Republic, and Congo (Brazzaville) Republic president Youlou governed territories lacking Gabon's natural wealth and depended heavily on French financial aid and on the local settlers in charge of their countries' only assets, mainly transportation and distribution facilities. Both tolerated political associates who enriched themselves openly and worked closely with the foreign business communities in Brazzaville and Bangui. Youlou indulged his extravagant personal tastes and ignored the poverty of the city's inhabitants while he bid for foreign support through an erratic and exaggerated anti-communism. Urban riots, led by unemployed students and workers, drove him and his colleagues out of the country in August 1963. A committee of civil servants and army officers, called the Mouvement National de la Révolution (MNR) and led by a former assembly deputy, Alphonse Massemba-Debat, quieted the civil disturbances and initiated the country's turn toward authoritarianism with the proclamation of a single-party state. Facing desperate revenue shortages and volatile city crowds, they sought foreign aid from so-called socialist countries and tried to reduce government expenditures. Cuts in the armed services budget brought an army mutiny in 1966, but the MNR's youth wing (the MNR-Jeunesse) rallied to the party and saved the government. It thereby acquired a strong voice in government circles that its leaders used to institute a radical foreign policy based on close relations with Cuba, the People's Republic of China, and other countries whose programs of national reconstruction seemed to offer answers to the Congo's hopeless economic plight. In the CAR, Dacko found himself losing power to corrupt political associates around him and so resurrected Boganda's alliance with the peasantry in an attempt to save his political career through rural development financed by foreign loans and domestic austerity. A trend toward personal authoritarianism accompanied these moves but was interrupted on New Year's Eve 1966, by an army rebellion in reaction to reduced military expenditures in Dacko's pared-down budget. The army chief of staff, Colonel Jean-Bedel Bokassa, assumed Dacko's place at the head of the government. In both countries parliamentary excesses had combined with persistent economic difficulties to force government austerity and a turn toward personal authoritatian rule that sparked army *coups d'état* and in the end consolidated unrepresentative forms of rule.[70]

The years 1959–65 in the Federation of Rhodesia and Nyasaland saw the release of Banda and Kaunda from prison, their return to politics at the head of militant nationalist parties, Banda's Malawi Congress Party (MCP) and Kaunda's United National Independence Party (UNIP), and the dissolution of the white-dominated federal government in 1963. Banda and the MCP assumed responsibility for Nyasaland's internal affairs and the country became independent as Malawi in 1964; Kaunda, the UNIP, and Northern Rhodesia followed a similar timetable to gain independence as Zambia. In Malawi, Banda almost at once asserted a highly personalized rule by dismissing the younger colleagues who had called him to Nyasaland in 1958 from their ministerial positions; he consolidated his power through close association with white southern Africa, where many Malawians continued to work as migrant laborers, and through reliance on a coterie of close friends and relatives. Chipembere responded to his dismissal with an ill-fated 1965 attack on Banda's strongholds but was driven out of the country, leaving Banda in full control of the government. Zambian independence brought Kaunda face to face with the urgent economic demands of the mineworkers and farmers that had voted the UNIP into power. At the same time he inherited from the days of the Federation a reliance on commercial and financial contacts south of the Zambezi. Kaunda chose to break these ties, in contrast to Banda's retention of Malawi's southern African connections, but received a serious setback with Southern Rhodesia's unilateral declaration of independence from Britain in 1965. Although vital Zambian rail links to sources of food and fuel ran through Rhodesia, Kaunda advocated the imposition of Pan-African economic sanctions against the rebel white regime in Salisbury and accepted the retaliatory Rhodesian embargo on shipments into Zambia and the consequent austerity imposed on his own nation.[71]

[70] For the former AEF, Guy de Lusignan, *French-Speaking Africa since Independence* (New York, 1969).

[71] Richard Hall, *The High Price of Principles: Kenneth Kaunda and the White South* (New York, 1969); Carolyn McMaster, *Malawi Foreign Policy and Development* (London, 1974).

Although independence passed by Angola in the early 1960s, the triumph of nationalism in neighboring territories shocked the Portuguese colony out of the lethargy that had enveloped it since the mid-nineteenth century. Tensions rose among both the would-be Angolan nationalists and the Portuguese in 1959 and 1960 as political police rounded up members of the largest of the covert African and mulatto political associations, the Movimento Popular para a Libertação de Angola (MPLA) in Luanda. When, late in 1960, a self-proclaimed prophet espousing vaguely nationalist rhetoric appeared in the cotton-growing regions of the middle Kwango, frightened Portuguese settlers set upon Africans in uncontrolled outbreaks of mob violence. African crowds stormed a Luanda prison in March 1961, and Kongo politicians living in Léopoldville but deeply involved in Kongo royal dynastic rivalries at São Salvador seized the opportunity presented by the breakdown in government authority to raise Angolan nationalist colors as the União das Populações de Angola (UPA) and to launch an uncoordinated and bloody assault on Portuguese in the coffee-growing region northeast of Luanda. Lisbon began a massive buildup of the Angolan army and slowly restored order while the MPLA leaders either retreated to a small mountainous enclave in the Dembos region not far from Luanda or plotted future engagements from residences in exile. The violence of 1961 subsided as the political police began a heavy-handed roundup of suspected nationalist sympathizers and the civil administration in Luanda initiated overdue programs to abolish the worst abuses present in the rural areas.

Authoritarian rule

The authoritarian regimes that took power in the former French colonies, the Congo (Kinshasa), and Malawi, in 1965 and 1966 have since consolidated their hold on the centers of power but have given little relief from rural misery. Bokassa sought a way out of the CAR's dependence on its resident settler community, but his solution to this long-standing problem increased his country's reliance on French financial aid just to keep the government bureaucracy running while it struggled to channel inadequate funds toward rural development. A politician without the means to satisfy his constituents' real needs, he resorted to spectacular demagoguery to camouflage his regime's underlying weaknesses.

Mobutu concealed continuing ties to European and American interests in the Congo beneath a veneer of Pan-Africanist rhetoric and *authenticité*, the latter a fabricated national culture and ethic proclaimed as a return to indigenous values that led to the renaming of the country and its protonymic river Zaïre in 1971, the abandonment of Léopoldian city designations (Stanleyville became Kisangani, Elizabethville became Lubumbashi, and so forth) and to the dropping of all Christian names by the citizens of Zaïre (Joseph Mobutu is now Mobutu Sese-Seko). His firm control of the army ended rural disorders and overcome the extreme regionalism left behind from Belgian days and evident in the secessions of 1960–63. A pervasive single political party reestablished close administrative supervision in the provinces, but only limited tangible benefits have flowed from centralized control. Mobutu has since been charged with the sort of personal aggrandizement, capricious use of force and intimidation, and collaboration with foreign interests that prompted Youlou's expulsion from the Congo Republic in 1963.

Across the river, Youlou's successors in Brazzaville persevered in their rapprochement with Marxist-Leninist regimes through a period of instability that ended with the 1969 proclamation of a République Populaire du Congo (Congo Peoples Republic) under a Congo Workers Party led by Mariem Ngouabi. The government, despite its socialist pronouncements and nomenclature, remained economically dependent on France and unable to respond meaningfully to the needs of the urban unemployed or the rural peasantry who remained poised to resort to violence; some reports indicated that strongarm tactics were used to maintain domestic order. In Gabon, Mba's successor and protegé, Albert Bongo, followed Mobutu's strategy of coupling consolidation of his single-party state to continued cooperation with European financial interests and well-publicized gestures intended to convey the impression of autonomy (he assumed the Muslim name of Omar in 1973). Banda did not alter Malawi's firm commitment to cooperate with Rhodesia and South Africa on whom his country's economy depended, nor did he relent in the firmness of his personal control.

Zambia resisted the trend toward authoritarian rule but the hardships brought by Kaunda's effort to break free of economic dependence on the south provoked domestic opposition that in 1973 and 1974 propelled the country in the direction already taken elsewhere in Equatorial Africa. Kaunda's economic policies yielded some successes; negotiations with Anglo-American and American Metal Climax (successor to the Rhodesian Selection Trust), for example, brought Zambia a fifty-one percent ownership of the copper industry and began to attack its "enclave" features by raising taxes on the remaining foreign ownership. But the higher costs of imports brought through Tanzania by pipeline, by road and, with the completion of the Tanzam Railway to the Indian Ocean at Dar-es-Salaam, by railroad as well, fell primarily on those least willing to afford them—the mineworkers and farmers in the cash economy who had also borne the brunt of colonial expenditures. An opposition political party formed to express their grievances in 1970 but Kaunda took the path blazed by other Equatorial African leaders faced with economic crises and domestic opposition; he arrested his political opponents and declared Zambia a one-party state with a greatly strengthened presidency to aid in the implementation of administrative rule.

Angola provided the only partial exception to the post-1965 return to authoritarianism in Equatorial Africa. In the aftermath of the confusion of 1961 both the Portuguese and the African liberation movements embarked on very different programs of social reconstruction. On the Portuguese side, Luanda implemented effective control over its rural administrators for the first time and provided a limited range of improvements to the rural population— wells, medical stations, roads, and schools. But these were accompanied by extensive resettlement of villages that introduced the sort of dislocations found elsewhere during the phase of mature colonial rule. On the African side, a restructured MPLA opened a new military front in southeastern Angola in 1965 and established schools, medical dispensaries, and rudimentary transportation and communication systems in its liberated areas. UPA, reformed as the Frente Nacional da Libertação de Angola (FNLA), issued similar claims for parts of northwestern Angola, but mass flight across the border into Zaïre by the area's Kongo residents cast doubt on the validity of their pronouncements. In 1966–67, a third movement, the União Nacional para a Independência Total de Angola (UNITA) established a small stronghold east of the upper

Kwanza and proclaimed achievements like those of the MPLA.[72] Military engagements continued into 1974 but the armed confrontation ground to a stalemate hindered by internecine struggles among, and within the competing liberation movements.

A 1974 *coup d'état* in Portugal sharply altered this situation by leading to a Portuguese withdrawal from Angola even more precipitate than Belgium's abandonment of the Congo in 1960; under pressure from all sides, MPLA, FNLA, and UNITA joined in a shaky transitional government with representatives of the new Lisbon regime and accepted a schedule calling for independence in November 1975. As European and neighboring African countries jockeyed for future influence over Angola's rich oil, iron, and diamond resources, the political leadership of the movements found their military forces increasingly difficult to control, and the underlying tensions spilled over into bloody fighting in Luanda and elsewhere. Independence Day found the MPLA in control of Luanda and the FNLA and UNITA mounting a joint assault on Angola's capital city, backed by Mobutu from Zaïre and South Africa from Namibia. The arrival of Cuban troops and munitions at Luanda turned the military situation in favor of the MPLA and led to widespread international recognition of the MPLA leadership, under President Agostinho Neto, as the government of independent Angola. Divisions within the new regime and sporadic guerilla attacks by defeated UNITA forces hindered reconstruction of the Angolan economy, once one of Equatorial Africa's richest, well into 1976.

Since neither independence nor the return to administrative rule changed the underlying conditions of life for most Equatorial Africans, attention had shifted between 1965 and 1974 to the Angolan liberation movements, especially the MPLA and UNITA, as the bearers of hopes for a significant departure from the continuities that had prevailed in Equatorial Africa from the early centuries through colonial rule and into independence. They alone premised their activities on the need to revitalize rural areas that lost their economic viability in the era of merchants and warlords. As the

[72] Gerald J. Bender, "The Limits of Counter-Insurgency: An African Case," *Comparative Politics*, 4, 3 (1972):331–60, and "Angola: History, Insurgency and Social Change," *Africa Today*, 19, 1 (1972):30–6.

indigenous kingdoms that once muffled the effects of the world market on the local lineages disappeared, colonialism reduced most villages to a defenseless dependence on forces they could not influence; UNITA and MPLA advocated locally autonomous economies under the control of peasant producers. They emphasized village participatory democracy as a solution to ancient tensions between small-scale local institutions and larger structures that persisted through the conflicts between kings and lineages, warlords and local populations, centralized colonial rule and rural impoverishment, national governments and rural rebels. Their village committees offered the only existing alternative to the expensive administrative bureaucracies developed by European governments and reestablished by authoritarian presidents in the independent nations. But independence in Angola seemed to have introduced there the same array of problems that kept other regimes from implementing the ideals proclaimed by the liberation movements while isolated in rural Angola. Rural poverty, urban violence, civilian-military tensions, and continuing foreign involvement in national politics threatened a speedy transition to authoritarian rule with as little relief for the rural areas as had prevailed elsewhere in Equatorial Africa.

Useful studies relevant to several periods of history in Equatorial Africa appear in T. O. Ranger, ed., *Aspects of Central African History* (New York: Heinemann, 1968), especially, for the modern period, John McCracken on "The Nineteenth Century in Malawi" and "African Politics in Twentieth-Century Malawi," and Andrew Roberts on "The Nineteenth Century in Zambia" and "The History of Twentieth-Century Zambia."